FOR
LOVE
OF
THE
DOLLAR

The Unnamed Press
P.O. Box 411272
Los Angeles, CA 90041

Published in North America by The Unnamed Press.

1 3 5 7 9 10 8 6 4 2

This book was originally published in Spanish by Joaquín Mortiz in 2006
as Por amor al dólar. It was released again in Spanish by Almadía en 2012.

ISBN: 978-1944700010

Library of Congress Control Number: 2016962849

This book is distributed by Publishers Group West

Cover design & typeset by Jaya Nicely

This book is a work of nonfiction.

We gratefully acknowledge that publication of this book was
made possible in part by the Mexican government and
the Programa de Apoyo a la Traducción (PROTRAD).

FOR LOVE OF THE DOLLAR

A PORTRAIT OF THE ARTIST AS AN UNDOCUMENTED IMMIGRANT

J.M. SERVÍN

Until we accept the fact that life itself is founded in misery*, we shall learn nothing.

Henry Miller

(Mystery*, in the original Miller quote)

INTRODUCTION
LIVING THE DREAM
BY DAVID LIDA

There are two prevalent narratives about undocumented Mexicans in the U.S. The first is a tale of hardship, sorrow, and danger — the story of the struggle of people on the fringes of towns and cities, unable to enjoy the rights and privileges of citizens; of endless days of monotonous work that nationals won't do any longer: landscaping, housekeeping, construction, scrubbing pots and pans, meat-packing.

The counter-narrative, repeated frequently by politicians and writers of pot-boiling thrillers about the drug trade, paints Mexicans without papers as cold-blooded criminals, "bad hombres," and "rapists," people who, if you so much as stand in their way, will shoot you between the eyes before tucking into a plate of enchiladas rojas.

However one-sided, there is a basic truth to both of these stories: The undocumented come from Mexico's most struggling social class. Otherwise, they wouldn't be undocumented. Immigration authorities have no problem issuing visas to Mexico's wealthiest citizens, but few of them have any desire to live in Gringolandia. Mexico's aristocrats stay away from the U.S. once they've earned their MBAs or other post-graduate degrees at Harvard or Stanford. After their commencement ceremonies, they prefer to return to Mexico, and plum jobs either in government, the private sector, or the family business, where on similar salaries to what they'd be earning in the U.S., scandalously cheap labor allows them to hire cooks, gardeners, maids and chauffeurs. I remember from the early 1990s a Mexican who referred to a gringo counterpart with a mix of contempt and disbelief: "He earns a hundred and fifty thousand dollars a year, and he mows his own lawn." This Mexican would travel to the U.S., but only to accompany his wife on trips to shopping malls in Houston and San Antonio.

J.M. Servín, author of *For Love of the Dollar*, is in a class by himself — at least as far as the literature of the undocumented is concerned. He is from the Mexican middle class. A little definition is in order. The term "middle class" in Mexico has nothing to do with what those same words mean in the U.S. (or at least nothing to do with what they used to mean before the economic crisis of 2008, when people in the U.S., whose salaries had been stagnating for twenty years, began to see an entire way of life disappear). The Mexican middle class, unlike the Mexican poor, does not struggle from day to day to put food in its mouth, but it definitely goes into panic mode at the end of each month when the bills are due. It is a social class that subsists on what would be considered slave wages in the U.S., and has few of the social benefits that middle-class people north of the border have traditionally taken for granted.

It's a social class that has been hammered by peso devaluations that have occurred consistently since the 1970s. When Servín was born, in 1962, the peso held steady at 12.5 to the dollar, and would continue to do so until 1976, when overnight it went to 22 to the dollar. By the early 1990s, it was at 3,400 to the dollar, before the president tried to "fix" the problem by lopping off three zeroes at the end of the currency.

Throughout these years, the elite and the impoverished tended to live more or less as they had throughout Mexican history, but the middle class struggled to keep afloat, when the falling oil prices, high inflation, no credit and rising interest rates became Sisyphean. Through much of the 1980s, Mexico's GDP grew at the rate of less than one percent per year, while inflation galloped at 100 percent annually. Many middle-class Mexicans who worked in both the private and public sectors lost their jobs, and began to emigrate to the U.S. by the thousands, to work in agriculture, construction, or maintenance. (One of these Mexicans was Servín's father, who found work supervising a jewelry workshop in Rosenberg, Texas.) Many of those who stayed behind resorted to work in the informal economy — parking cars, cleaning houses, or selling cigarettes and chewing gum at traffic intersections (when they weren't cleaning windshields or eating fire). These days, more than half of Mexico City earns its living informally. Servín came of age in the beginning of the 1980s, the start of what would become known to many in Mexico as "the lost decade."

"My parents could name all the pawnshops," Servín writes in *For Love of the Dollar*. "They transmitted their experiences to us as if by osmosis. 'Property should be used to get you out of sticky situations' was the family motto. My mother's children grew used to living on the installment plan. Filling our stomachs was the priority."

In the early 1990s, Servín went to New York on a tourist visa, which gave him permission to stay in the U.S. for a few months. He would remain there for seven years, minus a short stay in Ireland for what was essentially a drunken spree. *For Love of the Dollar* is a chronicle of those years, in which Servín did his best to ignore the prevalent social stereotypes of hangdog laborer or bloodthirsty drug dealer. Instead, he was inspired by some of his literary heroes, such as Louis-Fer-

dinand Céline, whose experiences as a young man in Africa,
Cuba and the United States (sometimes on medical missions
for the League of Nations), shaped the novels he would write
later in life. Or Nelson Algren, who came of age just as the
1929 stock market crash sent the world into the tailspin of
the Great Depression — and who spent some years hopping
freights around the U.S. (and did time in jail for stealing a
typewriter) before publishing his first book.

In contrast to the prevailing narratives, *For Love of the
Dollar* is a picaresque; a tale of adventure and misadventure,
as Servín wends his way through the Tri-state area. He finds
work in the kitchen of a restaurant in midtown Manhattan
(but not before spending a hundred and twenty dollars to ac-
quire a false Social Security number, in order to have the priv-
ilege of paying taxes on the six dollars an hour he earns). He
graduates to being a "nanny" for the rich brats of a suburban
family, where he helps himself to the liquor cabinet when no
one is looking. He also mows the lawns in an elite golf club,
and culminates his stay in the U.S. with a job pumping gas at
a Mobil station in Greenwich, Connecticut.

Throughout, Servín is skeptical, and at times downright
contemptuous, of his compatriots (including one who kisses
a crucifix around his neck each time someone gives him a dollar tip for cleaning a windshield). He writes:

> *The day laborers were never too interested in learning En-
> glish; they would let their bosses speak to them in chop-
> py, rude Spanish or through interpreters. Sometimes they
> wanted to learn, but they couldn't; at other times, they
> could, but there was always something better to do than
> go to classes...Sooner or later, the law of minimal effort
> would prevail. Single men would live crowded together
> in guesthouses or small rooms that were sometimes the
> property of their bosses. When they weren't working, they*

bummed around the house, lazing away the day. The most
obsessive ones saved up for ostentatious used cars, luxury
items, electrical apparatuses, or transactions with a coy-
ote...They would return to their countries each winter, and
they would return each spring to seasonal jobs, without
money and with hangovers that would last until summer.
They would complain, but the dollar's an addiction.

Unlike them, Servín revels in his status as an immigrant
in the shadows of his adopted country, living his version of
the American Dream: listening to James Brown records and
spending every cent he earns in dive bars, or on flasks of
whiskey and grams of cocaine to keep him warm on winter
nights in the gas station, or feeling up strippers in peep-show
booths in Times Square (just before that part of New York
was transformed into Disneyland). His quest for love and sex
most often ends in mishaps along the lines of a low-rent Henry Miller, in encounters with prostitutes, adulterous wives, or
waking up in a pool of vomit alongside other undocumented
Mexicans.

I'm not saying that Servín is the only Mexican who ever
crossed the border on a joyride. But as far as I know, he's the
only one who ever wrote a book about it. With a mordant eye,
he never loses sight of his social status and the Faustian bar-
gain the undocumented make along with their dollars. They
were:

...black and Latino workers, undesirable renters, but ready
to live by the highway and the interstate in a gloomy
neighborhood surrounded by factories, warehouses,
gas stations, and waste processing plants that attract-
ed opossum, squirrels, and skunks. The streets were rare-
ly traversed at night and, if so, only by people passing
through and looking for drugs in the nearby ghettos, all

*located next to the train station. Our awareness that we
lived in poor neighborhoods was consoled by the fact that
the power and water always ran, the streets were paved,
and that problems were taken care of quickly. The landlords asked for two months' rent in advance, for our work
phone numbers, and that we try to minimize our accents.
As a "favor," they wouldn't run the credit on the Social
Security number on the copy of our bank statement.*

Much has changed in the twenty or so years since Servín
left the U.S. and returned to Mexico. But some things stay the
same ad infinitum. Since the 1970s, U.S. politicians, talking
out of one side of their mouths, have spoken in accusing and
censorious terms of the "immigrant problem" in the U.S.,
while at the same time, out of the other side, exploiting those
same immigrants' willingness to work for low wages in their
communities (and pay taxes, sometimes at a higher rate than
the wealthy in those same communities). Now that the U.S.
has elected a president whose political platform was primar-
ily a screed against the undocumented, perhaps before long
we will regard *For Love of the Dollar* as a sentimental docu-
ment, some *nostalgie de la boue* from more carefree times.

David Lida

Mexico City, 2017

PROLOGUE

Norma picked up her bag from the desk and left the room, slamming the door. It wasn't the first time we'd argued, but it was the first time we'd insulted each other face-to-face. She had taken the liberty of snooping in my stuff and I caught her reading my stories. By way of apology, she admitted that they had a certain flair, but that they were corrosive and destructive. They reflected the worst of me without even trying. This type of "confessional" writing—that's what she called it—negated everything that Norma understood about "holding beliefs." But her fear of accepting the reasons she lived in an eighty-square-foot studio apartment was the real trigger for a squabble filled with bitter reproaches over the insinuations in my writing. Still, her complaints, as indignant as ever, didn't phase me; I'd made the call years ago to make no enemies, least of all my sister—our hatreds are chips off the same block.

As far as I'm concerned, all of humanity's acts are plagued by hatred and disappointment. Norma is ruled by her visceral opinions not only about me, but about all of those who surround her. Hatred, a much more sincere feeling than "love," is the piston of rebelliousness, the only way of denying misers and scoundrels any respect. If we didn't have the option of sugarcoating it with irony, the streets would be filled with execution walls and scaffolds.

Accepting hatred as a part of our essence keeps us afloat above the scared and resentful masses—whom Norma secretly loathes—those who are incapable of hating, who just keep themselves busy with any old trinket in their hands. A mass of unhappy people hounded by hunger and poverty from all corners of the world. Mexicans, as always, anguishing and puppet-like. Submissive, swindled, apathetic, and yet agonizing over little things. Loyal to their tyrants and to their sweet Virgen de Guadalupe. But if we were to position ourselves beyond hatred, we might aspire to the freedom of assuming responsibility for our decisions without laying the blame on others.

That's how I was trying to sum up the contradictions in my fragmented culture and my daily experiences. It proved pointless to highlight the motives behind what I rejected and what I held on to. Norma was one of the few day laborers I knew who, at least until that moment, would open up to me about more than just the typical problems of people like us. She left the TV blaring as the final evidence of her furious presence in the room, then her high heels hastily descended the stairwell of the house on Alexander Avenue.

It had been a brief yet intense argument, leaving me exhausted. I turned off the television and lay down in bed. The ceiling fan looked like a vulture circling above its prey. The whipping blades were not enough to ease the tense and sticky atmosphere, nor to shoo away the flies sneaking in through some hole in the open window's screen.

PART I
THE BRONX IS BURNING

CHAPTER ONE

In which...
the Artist arrives in the Bronx on the Fourth of July...
the Artist's sister becomes the Artist's roommate...
the Artist learns about brownstones...the landlord keeps
an open mind about different ethnicities...the Artist
gets to know the other boarders.

You could relax in the South Bronx only if you agreed to give up silence. Its residents formed the core of a refined version of barbarism within a society that was as opulent as it was inequitable. On the streets of the United States, enough rifles and handguns were in circulation to arm all of Mexico and Central America. A few thousand people died from gunfire each year, many of whom lived in the Bronx, but that's saying nothing about the incessant influx of undocumented immigrants, like my sister and myself, nor about their daily experiences. It was a territory where nobody, absolutely nobody, walked without looking over his or her shoulder.

I arrived in the Bronx on the Fourth of July 1993 with nothing to lose, so I was able to drift along without thinking too much about it. My sister had arrived three years before me at the same time of year. We both immigrated in an airplane, with tourist visas. For myself, the most difficult thing was borrowing some money in order to open a savings account and trick the U.S. embassy in Mexico City into thinking I really had enough cash to be a legitimate tourist, while maintaining the attitude of someone who couldn't care less. In Mexico, I had been unemployed for a year after quitting my last job as a butcher in a swank restaurant. I would start in the evenings and finish at dawn, returning home after a two-hour trip in a small bus following routes designed expressly for those of us on nightshift schedules, mostly at restaurants and clubs. Exhaustion traveled in the packed convoys, as well as a resentment that, with each shove upon getting off, getting on, or grabbing a seat, threatened to erupt into an all-out brawl, which the majority longed for as an outlet for their frustrations. Even though we recognized one another from the commute, there was always a reason to suspect that the other guy held the worst intentions. Many traveled plastered or stoned in order to catch some shut-eye before getting home. In those years, Coca-Cola had yet to become one of the basic food groups of many day laborers; but even then I experienced an intense love-hate relationship with the beverage and with my weak will. I was reckless about destroying myself and a coward when it came to assuming any responsibility about my predicament.

Before leaving Mexico, my only distractions were reading and the fading love of a woman who fed on her obsessive fears through me. At the slightest provocation, I would recite to her from memory something from Louis-Ferdinand Céline that always helped me during my all-hours journey through the city: "Travel is very useful and it exercises the imagination. All the rest is disappointment and fatigue. Our own journey is entirely imaginary. That is its strength."

I had never come up with any specific goals apart from having a few bucks to keep myself afloat. In reality, far from the tragedies marking the routes of the average day laborer, my perception of work rested on the experiences of my father in Rosenberg, Texas, twenty-three years ago. He never complained or mentioned any insults or abuse.

From the Bronx, Norma wired some money to Mexico to help me set something aside for the plane ticket. She did so by subletting half of a large room she rented for $350 per month in one of those four-story redbrick vertical houses called *brownstones*. Sometime in the not too distant past, the bleak houses of the South Bronx housed working-class Irish, Italians, and Jews. Now they were rented out as tenements to inhabitants who were mainly black or Latino. One house could mix entire families, including different nationalities, equipped with their own prejudices, traditions, and nostalgia. The substance of daily anecdotes in the neighborhood was picaresque and tragic.

Initially, Norma and I got along well enough because our work schedules made it impossible for us to run into each other during the week. In Mexico, Norma had gotten married to and divorced from an egocentric and alcoholic painter who had taken their daughter and fled to Italy. At the height of this crisis, Norma met Rose, our landlady, when Rose was visiting Mexico to exhibit her sculptures, neither losing nor gaining any fame, in a gallery far from the capital. Norma's husband had arranged the contacts and a place to stay in Mexico; he used to travel abroad using the same strategy. Rose was a slender fortysomething whose parents were Italian. She was as an assistant principal at a Manhattan art school and bought the house on the urging of her second husband, a Nuyorican with a top-ranking position on the city's Council on the Arts. After a few years, when their divorce was finalized, Rose kept the house. She put up all types of nutcases, artists, and loners who worked in the arts and who would quickly move to safer neighborhoods at the first opportunity.

Despite our origins, Rose believed in keeping an open mind about different ethnicities, something that was important to maintain in the South Bronx. Norma and I piqued the curiosity of our fellow renters, who had neuroses like ours, but were all gringos: Rose's much younger boyfriend, Joe; Sandra Parker, her antisocial confidante and accomplice; Mark, a son from Rose's first marriage; and Mark's wife, Carol.

Joe moved in shortly before I did. He was tall and well-built, like some Faulknerian farmer with a severe poker face. If a murder had been committed in the house, Joe would have been the prime suspect. When he opened his mouth, it was only to eat. He and Norma couldn't stand each other. Joe's quiet insolence amused me; he didn't compel others to be polite or engage in chitchat, even when he prepared many of the Sunday suppers—almost always a roasted chicken with potatoes or a lasagna—when Rose and Norma played the role of little sisters getting the family together. At the table, Joe shoveled in enormous mouthfuls while hiding behind the newspaper. Norma always accused him of being a parasite, the thorn in her side. He knew this, and when Norma was about to explode over some crisis regarding household chores and his lack of accountability, Joe would shut her down with a "Hello. How you doin'?" while on his way to the refrigerator, where he would wolf down sandwiches and defiantly stare deep into a cabinet.

Our room on the top floor was separated from Sandra's with a shared bathroom. Sandra, always dressed in black, was a fan of Elvis and cats, especially her own: Graceland. Sandra left lit cigarettes beside her plate during Sunday suppers, the only day when she would sit at the table with everyone else, the feeble and curling smoke protecting her from the bombardment of intrusions on her life. Everyone felt they had the right to give her advice or to fix her up with a love interest.

Upon returning from work, she often bit the tip of her dark glasses while listening to the messages on the answering machine. Then she rushed upstairs to her room to sit in front of the window with a view of the backyard. She would spend hours like that with a sad look in her eyes, her gaze lost among the bricks of the neighboring wall and its tapestry of ivy, which definitively announced the turning of each season. While petting Graceland, Sandra would chain-smoke with a glass of brandy. Slight and silent and approaching forty, she had watched her youth get bogged down during the Cold War. In an enormous trunk with a mirror were stored imitation jewelry and clothes dating from that period, which she used on special occasions.

At night I would go to the kitchen for a beer and sit down in the dining room in order to admire the ancient lineage of the house with its high ceilings, antique rugs and furniture, enormous altarpieces on the walls, and bright hardwood floor. The bookshelves were one more decoration; no one was interested in the books on mysticism or interior decoration, nor the novels penned by women. Rose had inherited some of the furniture from her parents, and she was careful about keeping it in a dusty and careless state. Someone else would clean it. Norma, for example. The house enclosed an atmosphere of stale gentrification cut off from the danger of the streets and its disturbing cacophony.

Sometimes Sandra came down from her room with a bottle of brandy in one hand and Graceland in the other, pressed against her plum-shaped breasts, and we would talk.

"How's work going?"

"I guess it's okay," I answered. "At least I haven't set myself on fire."

I was alluding to the giant stove at the restaurant where I had recently found a job.

"Like a bonze monk?"

"Let's say that I don't have a religious bent."

"That's...good...surviving is what matters, or isn't that so?"

"Yes. Keeping my mind occupied."

She would return to the long stretches of silence by preparing doubles with ice while softly laughing at a joke that she wouldn't share with anyone. We were the only self-confessed alcoholics at the house. We would sporadically hear arguments or moaning from Mark and Carol's basement studio, where a sweet odor of marijuana would escape whenever Joe was there playing video games with Mark.

Sandra and I talked about experiences invariably alluding to infectious diseases or mental illness (she tirelessly read the Marquis de Sade). The rest of our conversation was about stupid people and drugs. Sandra was an autodidact. She dabbled with poetry, engravings, and photocopies from a Xerox machine. She liked to reproduce faces indefinitely, juxtaposing them against one another until deforming the original image with dark and carcinogenic colors, like those one notices on the streets when dawn starts to absorb the light from marquees and neon signs. She would print some of her poems, which almost always began with an answerless question or with words like *death, loneliness,* or *boredom.* She would also copy photos of her face; she gave one to me for a marginal tabloid that I edited in Mexico City. I was tempted to send them as photographs to the section where anonymous people formed part of a fictitious police file. Lombrosian art, I called it. But the day I arrived in the Bronx, I also cut all ties to my recent past for good. I had no reasons to drag it into the light now that I was facing a new life. With my departure from Mexico, I decided to end my apprenticeship as a loser; I was now set on humbly assuming myself as one, and without making a fuss or any highfalutin justification—as simply and as plainly as someone who recognizes his juicy family history, filled with unscrupulousness and conflicts, and, as a result, someone capable of living in the here and now.

Without any reservations, I understood the uselessness of presenting myself as a "writer" in surroundings where only English was spoken or among illiterate day laborers. I had spent five years trying to finish a novel based on my experiences as an adolescent among dogfighters, but my efforts proved to be those of an ugly bird without feathers, clumsy and hungry. I still didn't have any books published, and talking about the future was like jerking off while thinking about a woman I hadn't met yet. On top of that, I was trying to avoid a situation in which one of Rose's friends—for the most part, they were all art students with identity problems, or civil servants, or teachers—might take advantage of the occasion to show off his or her advantageous sensitivity with "I paint . . ." or "Personally, I like literature; actually, I have some stories. Have you ever read...?" I had many years under my belt in dealing with those empty titles belonging to elegance, financial solvency, position, and prestige that are so pleasing to imposters. I had nothing to do with all of that. (And yet my sister's indiscretion and critique as a tasteful reader infuriated me, and I—who so appreciated silence—had defended my lofty ambitions by screaming.)

Some photos of Sandra ended up decorating part of a wall in my room. In each one she had a cigarette dangling from a hand or the corner of her lips. Sandra's character was like the teetering between dawn and daybreak: those moments when one hesitates between running home from the light, or sprawling out on a bench while letting the drunkenness wear off, smoking wearily and absorbed, like after fucking a stranger. With Sandra, you never knew when to light one last cigarette before going to bed, drunk but still lucid. That moment could arrive inopportunely: Sandra would leave without saying good-bye, a sudden sobriety overtaking her.

I learned that after various weeks of identical nights. With booze and Marlboros to spare, I waited in the kitchen thinking that Sandra had gone to take a piss. I finished the brandy, most of the cigarettes, without pausing to think if

Sandra was actually gone for good; finally, I went to my room, juggling the glass up a staircase that felt steeper than usual. I crossed the second-floor landing where the largest room was, and I heard the labored breathing of Rose, as if she weren't sleeping and Joe was suffocating her with a pillow. Upon reaching the top floor, I saw the bar of light from beneath Sandra's door and heard the sound of country music guitar from Sandra's record player. I paused in front of her door for a brief moment, mentally re-creating the interior's scene: Sandra smiling drunk while swinging her hips in front of her trunk's mirror. Then I continued on my way.

Without turning on the lamp, I shrugged off my clothes like I had a hand tied behind my back and, tottering, threw myself into bed, forgetting about the full glass of brandy as well as the cigarette smoldering in the ashtray. I had a hard-on, but it wasn't because of Sandra. Or maybe it was. But only for the ample illusion instigated by drunken binges in a place I found strange and evocative. The curtains of white cloth filtered the sandy brilliance from the lamppost beneath the window. For a long time, I let myself drift along on my imagination and the almost imperceptible strumming of the soothing electric guitar as it played a Texan version of "Blue Moon." And that's how I fell asleep.

CHAPTER TWO

In which...the Artist gets to know his neighborhood.

The dilapidated constructions in the Bronx, some of them occupied by the homeless, have the appearance of an inevitable catastrophe: fire, demolition. Bricked-up doors and windows enclose chapters of gloomy epics in the country of the easy buck.

To my sorrow, the Bronx revived unbearable memories. I had already educated myself via an abundance of myths extracted from movies, music, and literature that combined the sordidness of my origins with the opulent culture of the States. Something soothed me; I knew that while I was in the United States, I would never again wear shoes patched together with tape or clothing from the swap meet. In the United States I would be a first-class poor man.

The few whites who lived in the Bronx, like Rose and her other tenants, were like a rash on the dark skin of the neighborhood. Despite my few ventures into the city, I knew from first sight that I had in my grasp all the resources of a society where efficiency was the norm. From the subway that ran twenty-four hours, churches for every creed, schools, libraries, nightclubs, bars, and restaurants serving ethnic food, to alcohol, drugs, weapons, and well-equipped police, the Bronx confined us to territories defined by the fear of disturbing the general indifference.

$

The argument with Norma left me feeling restless and with a parched mouth. I went to the store and avoided making any noise to not get tangled up in a conversation with someone from the household. I crossed the street. I bought three thirty-two-ounce Colt 45s and two packs of cigarettes: I was thinking about Sandra. The store stayed open for sixteen hours every day of the week. Behind the counter there was always one of four Dominican brothers who had saved money for thirty-odd years to become the owners of the most important store for blocks around. They were thinking of investing their savings into remodeling the business into a supermarket. "Self-service is more relaxed, *tú sabe*," the sour-faced youngest brother with horse teeth would say. He would pretend to reach for the automatic pistol hidden behind the counter when he caught some odd behavior in the convex mirror at the back of the store. Sometimes we would crack jokes, and I obligingly accepted whenever he called me "bro," as I thought that that would eventually let me run a tab. No such thing.

By the corner on 138th Street, a group of old Puerto Ricans and Mexicans would gather. They would drink beer and slap down dominoes on a folding metal table. In the entryway of their building they had a tape recorder that played Javier Solís. I approached them to observe the game. They seemed to ignore my presence, and then with a know-it-all air they would hum the melody upon making a play. All of a sudden one of the Puerto Ricans addressed me without taking his eyes off the pieces.

"What the hell's wrong? Too hot?"

"Somewhat."

"Go ahead and grab a beer."

They called him Papi. He pointed to the bag at his feet. I bent down to take out a can. I took the beer and pretended to be interested in the game. Papi had been the owner of a barbershop and a bazaar that sold trinkets, and he was one of the area's patriarchs. He loved boxing and borrowing money; he'd often visit Rose to talk about his son, the high-class cultural functionary who hadn't appeared on those streets since the divorce.

"You from Mexico?" one asked.

"That's right."

"Lots of Mexicans 'round here. Nice folk, ain't that so?"

"Yep."

The Mexican they were referring to coughed after answering, focusing on his dominoes.

"Take it slow, bro," Papi said to me. "Savor the beer. The store's nearby. And besides, if we run out, we'll send you to get more."

After the cackles, the slapping of dominoes on the table continued. I offered them a Colt and they all took a sip. When it got back to me, it was almost empty. I finished it off. I stayed for a long while, and nobody said another word to me. Belches. Suddenly, Papi looked at me from the corner of his eye. Neighbors walked by with an attitude as if they were the only ones on the street. Almost all of them were black. Some entered the store, others paused at the corners, looked around, while some others would run by or communicate shouting. Men and women glistened with sweat and aromatic creams. The women would wear short pants stretched tight across their asses and suggestive blouses without sleeves, braless; the men ambled about bare chested, some of them rubbing their bellies. The heat on that asphalt beach was a good enough motive to take out one's bad mood on the kids and curse from one sidewalk to another. The Mexicans let fly insults in a well-rehearsed English learned from the reproaches of others. One of them asked me a question in a falsetto vernacular. He spoke with a hint of a ranchero's nasality. He sported boots and a hat, which helped transform him into an imported urban cowboy who would never return to wearing huaraches and a straw hat.

"What part of Mexico you from?"

"From the capital."

Two of my countrymen standing nearby groaned in unison while remaining focused on the game.

The game continued in silence. When it finished, I said good-bye, and everyone murmured a "see you later" without removing their gazes from the dominoes.

In the kitchen, I opened a beer and put the other one in the refrigerator. While going up to my room, I savored the coolness trapped in the staircase. The white walls and the high ceiling helped with the ventilation. I sat at my desk in order to go over my drafts. I wanted to have some fun by writing something that would contradict my sister's accusations— that's to say, something grandiloquent, something that could be passed off as committed and poetic. But I gave up, once again confronting my own notebooks filled with false starts. Yet another battle between duty and desire.

$

The streets at the start of the evening changed into a furious soundboard. Sirens. Noises and music wove links, at times imperceptible due to the enraged tirades of rappers. It all seemed like an invocation to tribal identities that responded with delight to the street's schizophrenia adorned with graffiti. Tone and rhythm with resonations inspired by Lucky Cienfuegos and Miguel Piñero: those capos of the underworld's poetry. Odors of fried food, sea, incense, and the immense farts from smokestacks browned the summer breeze. International flags fluttered from windows, entryways, and cable TV dishes that adorned immigrant hierarchies. The Bronx and its shouting. People posturing from fear. Jokesters.

People warning you. Where the devil prowls at all hours is where the crime sheets publish the most-read epitaphs.

I would perceive a neighborhood that didn't progress: it lurched. From one form of barbarism to another, it purified in its own special way an implacable, productive fundamentalism. The immigrant hordes surrendered themselves to it wholly, with customs from the old country and other stubborn habits. Living under the same law—eye for an eye, tooth for a tooth—the interpretations of God's word separated and singled out folks. If advanced societies organized themselves through exclusion, the Bronx was a tumor to dig out. Here, where one could see the distant skyscrapers, one had a free pass to the violence of machismo.

Back then, I had no idea how many months would pass by before I served my time as an immigrant.

$

I awoke at dawn, hungry and hungover. I glanced at the clock on the nightstand. In two hours they would open the store. The hurried clacking of heels resounded from the street, and in the distance, dogs barking, electronic drum beats, and car alarms. I paused for a moment, wondering if Norma had returned to say good-bye to me but, upon seeing me sound asleep, had opted to not do so. She had saved enough during the year in order to go to Italy and visit her daughter. Norma worked as a nanny in a town next to the Bronx, up north, in the county of Westchester. It was a place that was immaculate, peaceful, and desolate—the area where wealthy white people lived. She believed that a brother who "wrote" would make her stay in the United States less lonely. She had read only a few music reviews that I wrote early on for a newspaper in the capital. It's certain that she assumed I hung out with important people. Almost all of her information came from letters my other brothers had sent her, and they knew about as much as she did. She presumed that I was working on a highway that would get me far away from the slums and mediocrity. She never imagined that the majority of my writing was a result of all that. She also didn't know that the majority of the material had been rejected for that reason, among others. Plus, she hadn't seen my file with clippings and photos from the lurid crime pages. She believed what she tried best to believe and feared digging any deeper. Nothing but pure intuition. We never talked about me.

CHAPTER THREE

**In which...the landlord's son is revealed to be the
Video Game Hero...Reluctant Roommate...
and Protector of the Realm.**

Mark spent several days without appearing in the Bronx.
Rose shared this information with me while we had lunch in
the backyard. Sandra hadn't mentioned this during our recent
light-night sessions, and I didn't notice the usual noise that
once emanated from the basement studio was now gone. No
more complaints about someone plundering the groceries.
Until then I hadn't understood Norma's taciturn way when it
came to waiting for news. Despite everything, the atmosphere
in the house was now agreeable; the dog days no longer
penetrated walls and windows, and Joe and Norma weren't
at each other. An ideal circumstance for weekends, without
a doubt. Sandra would stay in her room, and we probably
wouldn't see her until dinner. Rose exaggerated her concerns,
but she was shaken up enough about the matter to not even
take her dosage of Valium.

Mark was all grown up, twenty-eight years old, married
to a Californian woman who gave off airs as an intellectual.
She was working at Condomania until she could land a better
gig. With a BFA in interior design, money wasn't something
that worried Carol a whole lot, especially not while her parents
continued to send her a monthly check to cover her expenses.
Mark preferred expensive restaurants. His friendly look,
clean-shaven features, and gift of the gab as a salesman were

his calling cards for that moment when he would eventually ask if there were any openings for waiters.

"He's probably with his friends, you know him. Have you called around?" I said in order to reinforce Rose's suspicions and assumptions, before going upstairs to take a shower, feeling woozy from the tedious chatter from someone who needed someone else to take care of her own problem.

All of Mark's friends lived in Brooklyn and he spent the majority of his time with them, except for those moments when they would get together in his studio in order to play video games or watch the Oscars, all of them dressed up like movie stars. Mark always chose Robert De Niro in his role from *The Godfather*. Joe would dress up as a John Wayne type of cowboy, while Carol dressed up as Ingrid Bergman in *Casablanca*. The cast from *The Rocky Horror Picture Show* delivered to your door.

Mark liked smoking pot with Joe. Without speaking too many words, they understood each other. When Mark would bring his friends over, Joe would go downstairs to the basement studio. They loved pizza, fruity soft drinks, and chocolate, and apart from video games and computers, they had exchanged basketballs and bicycles for bongs.

Mark always had a lot of excuses to not be at home. They almost always had to do with job hunts or culinary night classes. The last time, he had signed up for a course at an institute for French pastries. He dropped out after three months, and with a loan from his mother, he opened a pastry shop on the outskirts of New York, close to where his maternal grandparents lived. He found Carol and they spent almost a year as his grandparents' tenants. When they returned to the Bronx, Mark was depressed and irritable, and Carol stopped talking to all of us. Rose's anger dissipated not too long after, though her savings had been depleted from the parties, rental items, burned cakes, cake decorations, and equipment with which they'd started the business.

Mark was confident that he would soon be a prosperous restaurateur, or at least that's what he would claim each time he started a new job as a waiter.

Carol wanted to believe him, and, with Rose, she would spend entire afternoons knitting and making plans for the future. Mark wasn't a nobody. He wasn't another one of those under-the-table guys in kitchens filled with Latinos and Asians, nor a hired hand working during the winter season. He was a full-fledged citizen of the United States and proud of being Italian American. That's what Rose and her daughter-in-law reasoned animatedly, yet guarding their words in front of "foreigners."

Mark had promised Carol that she would soon be the owner of a gift boutique with products she designed, while he ran a trattoria in Brooklyn—"Just give me some time," he would say. But for the meantime, he would excuse himself before leaving the house and looking for his crew. He was the leader, the only one married, and the only one whose mother had lent him his own studio. He was also the only one ever suspected of pilfering cash from Rose's purse. Demands met the conditions present: a cute house, all expenses included, and a cute wife. Moreover, his buddies revered him for being the best at video games.

As for the rest of us, his best quality was his frequent absence.

Everything was going well for Mark; the only hitch in his plan was his return to the Bronx at night. Since childhood, it bugged him to be surrounded by "loud and aggressive" neighbors who never said a word to him. But, as for now, there was nothing he could do. His mother's hospitality helped him avoid paying astronomically high rent for apartments the size of a walk-in closet outside of the Bronx. Mark had confessed to me once how the forty-five-minute ride from Brooklyn made each hair on his body stand up when he reached Ninety-Sixth Street. From thereon, only crazy blacks and Latinos boarded the cars.

"Oh, man, there are so many!" he would say while counting with his fingers, pretending to be astonished. Rap music, eyes reddened from drugs, and everything else dark, *really* dark, and then he would unleash a sardonic cackle that made his mother uncomfortable.

Mark had no motivation to connect with his neighbors. They made him feel ashamed. Luckily enough, the police station was on the corner. With just a shout, they would be there for him, ready to protect a U.S. citizen. Joe was always on his side, even though Mark would discreetly chide his mother for having chosen a much younger partner. "Jesus, Mom," Mark would complain whenever his demands weren't met.

The South Bronx was an unbearable Babel with hostile neighbors. It was a rare event when Mark went to the store for groceries. He preferred to pick among things in the fridge and the community cupboard. He loved my Colombian coffee. Whenever possible, my sister would advise Rose to get her son in line. Mark thought it reckless that Rose had rented a room to two Hispanics, but he nevertheless convinced my sister to let him borrow her car. Once he disappeared with it for two days; the police stopped him, and he didn't say a thing about that. When the $200 fine came in the mail, my sister stopped all loans and borrowing forever.

"It's nothing personal, Mark, but she doesn't like lending money for breaking the law while driving drunk."

Mark didn't say anything else. No one believed his excuses, which weren't very original. Eventually no one cared about his petty theft when it came to groceries or forgotten change in the pockets of jackets hanging by the foyer.

Mark would always say, "You'll pay for this," which clashed with his ingenuous smile. *"Patience!"* he would yell at Carol when they argued in the studio, especially whenever he had disappeared for some days. "I have the right to have some fun, don't I?" was the way he would finish off his act of being offended, which lasted for a few hours.

$

Alexander Avenue at night. Anyone you looked in the eye for more than five seconds would assume you were challenging him to a fight.

Once, Mark had to learn this the hard way. It couldn't be avoided, as the guys were only a few feet from the subway. Mark had exited from the subway a bit before dawn. They had broken into Norma's car, and they had taken out the dashboard with screwdrivers and by pulling on it to snap off the wires. Meanwhile, one of the thieves had opened all four doors in order to help the others with their undertaking. Mark wasn't sure if he had witnessed all of this from the moment they had started. After all, it was the car that was no longer going to be lent to him, the car that he could have used upon returning from Brooklyn and with fewer risks.

They were trying to turn over the engine of the modest white Subaru with some miles on it, the typical sort of jalopy that poor workers with modest incomes used. They couldn't get it to start. They pulled out a stereo, which had cost a hundred bucks from a nearby Caldor. They had cracked the windshield while trying to take apart the dashboard. The four Mexicans from the neighboring house were no professionals. They didn't even care about the ruckus they were making, nor that their own children were keeping watch nearby, at the foot of the house.

Mark found himself in the midst of their gazes. The sudden silence only confirmed that they recognized and loathed each other. An ambulance siren whizzed down Willis Avenue, parallel to Alexander end to end. Mark tried to, but couldn't, pretend that he had taken the wrong way, yet his reflexes urged him onto the stairs of his house. He had one hand stuck in his pants pockets. House keys. Fear confused him. It didn't occur to him that in order to enter his studio he had to go down the stairs, not go up, and now he had to return to those icy gazes of the thieves, who were still watching him. He walked down, as if he were out to buy the newspaper. Before stepping on the sidewalk, he searched his breast pocket. There they were, chained to the tweezers in the shape of a pistol that he used to smoke roaches. The Mexicans surrounded him: grimy, long-haired Pygmies, shirtless and with their pants sagging.

"You shouldn't do that," he said, trapped by the circumstances. His voice broke despite how hard he tried to remain calm.

The thieves looked at him one last time. Then after telling him to fuck his mother in Spanish, and with their chins pressed against their chests, they ran off carrying the spare tire and a canvas bag.

Mark let out a gasp of relief. He had scared them off. He looked at the police station and then at the patrol cars, the motorcycles, and the cars used by plainclothesmen. They would park out front in some reserved spaces by the same sidewalk in front of his house and the police station. Laughter erupted from some building. He placed his hand again in his shirt pocket to feel the smoothness of the key ring: a good replica of a Smith & Wesson used in the Old West.

He walked down the steps leading to the studio, and while passing by the trash cans, he put their lids on. Carol was asleep on the sofa in front of the TV. He gave her a kiss soured by whiskey, chocolate, and weed, but she didn't wake up. He undressed while humming the theme to *Top Cat*, his favorite cartoon. He had a glass of milk, and before getting into bed, he looked at his Top Cat pupils. Without saying anything more, he went to sleep, exhausted.

The light from the entryway upstairs turned on at that moment. Rose and my sister opened the door, alarmed. They didn't see anyone, and Norma found that her car had been broken into. Shortly after, Rose, wearing a robe, accompanied her to file a report with the police. Norma made a statement, and in return, the sergeant said there was nothing more they could do and that she should go back to sleep. Rage kept Norma up all night. Even in my sleep, I could hear her muttered curses against the United States.

In the morning, when I went down for some coffee, my sister was having breakfast with Rose and Mark. Norma barely touched her waffles drowning in maple syrup, listening to the story with an icy gaze. He could never explain exactly why he didn't call the police.

CHAPTER FOUR

In which...all of these barrios look alike...Leo the Homeless Man dies because..."We'll never find out who did this."

Up and down 138th Street, from east to west, travel all types of the condemned on their way to hell. Day and night, hollering and braggadocio rouse them. On each corner, in empty lots and abandoned buildings, there's a collector for the devil. All types of subnormal people, convalescents, maniacs, and old folk incapable of walking down to the street on their own lean out the windows; saved from imprisonment, they restlessly gaze at the action. The windows air out the matriarchs wearing hair rollers, the tireless uteruses of what's often called the "barrio." The common rhythm of life here is a déjà vu of my adolescence. The people live with the same resentments and fears as those who were my neighbors during fifteen years in small units, tenements, and cinder block rooftop huts in Mexico City: the poor and the even poorer among lewd and vicious repeat offenders.

All these barrios look alike. They're the precipices hanging over the hopes for one's well-being. The fear they inspire in me doesn't minimize my morbid curiosity. For years, it has been the only stimulant that I've had to return home to as I lock myself inside and read. That's how I learned to live with myself. Alexander Avenue crosses 138th. The corners are occupied by a Catholic church, the police station with the subway entrance next to it, a housing complex tower, and a somber brick building with fire escapes zigzagging down its facade. An Irish bar has survived on the ground floor. I doubt that the dingy cardboard and neon four-leaf clovers hanging in the window and from the walls inside have brought anyone luck. They're the nationalistic fetish of a ruddy-faced bartender who supplies bilingual sots with beer and bourbon. The church takes in the Latinos, mainly Mexicans, as well as the few black folk who are not evangelicals, Seventh-Day Adventists, or Muslim. The devoutness of Mexicans is so intense there's even a mural of the dark-skinned Virgin in the back patio of the church; every twelfth of December, a pilgrimage starts there and ends at Saint Patrick's Cathedral in Manhattan in order to sing a birthday praise to the Virgin of Guadalupe: the greatest and most passionate patroness known on the East Coast for workers and their daily grind in kitchens, factories, and warehouses.

The cult of blood also shares those same corners.

$

Leo died only because he was a sick, old man who no longer cared about danger. He dragged his feet without taking his gaze off from the crack of survival that grew wider and wider beneath him. His supermarket cart rolled against the sidewalk, spilling tin cans, blankets, and winter clothing. He didn't need three gunshots to the rib cage, but no one thinks about that when pulling the trigger. The gaunt body of that bum probably gave up after the first shot. On that evening he was the target of an unknown suspect who, according to an eyewitness, had been slowly cruising around Willis Avenue and 138th, one of the crew members aboard a Ford sedan.

I reached the bloody bulk, avoiding the silent statues gathered there and staring at the scene in disbelief. The moment he was shot, I was at the corner store buying beer and cigarettes, and chatting with the grocer about the Saturday boxing matches shown on a Spanish-language TV station. We had changed the topic of discussion when he mentioned how a crime had been solved by a detective with a Dominican background and who was the son of one of the grocer's friends, who had saved all of his earnings to buy a house on one of the beaches in his country.

The dry and quick bursts reminded me of the sound made when smashing an inflated paper bag. Then there were some hysterical shrieks drowned out by squealing tires. The music coming from nearby apartment windows slowly filled the stillness that followed the shooting. The grocer and I stayed quiet while looking at each other in shock, and then, without saying good-bye, I walked outside, ignoring the warnings. I went along guided by the pedestrians who passed me, running in the direction of the cadaver as if they were spurred along by a stampede, nearly knocking down the police officers who were exiting the station to investigate. As always when there's a death in the street, the carrion eaters arrived before the ones trying to prevent things like that.

After a few minutes, the street filled up with gawkers, and shouts were heard as if the people had woken up from a heavy sleep while something interesting was occurring. The local drunk, the sickly woman panhandling outside the stores, the thug, the scaredy-cat, the pimp, the cholo, and the trickster surrounded the cadaver while making comparisons with other local tragedies. They pushed each other, pointed, even laughed. We wanted life to provide something novel to talk about.

I felt an emptiness in my stomach as if I were fasting. I saw a body stretched out on the asphalt. I couldn't understand if the face looked waxen because of life or death. On the corner, the police were sharing their report with some other patrolmen in front of the station, the very same ones who had just taken control of the tumult with choreographed coldness and efficiency.

"As far as I can see, we'll never find out who did this," a passerby experienced with the law of the jungle pronounced.

"Well, what are you doing here then?" one of the cops retorted, defending himself from the implied critique.

For me, this confirmed how simple it was for one to meddle in the affairs of another person without that person being able to stop it. I asked a few questions, and I stood near the police officers and the experts to hear their comments, and I was a few inches from a dead man without having to be dead in order to do so. All of that without needing to flash any credentials. On similar occasions, fear shook my resolve as a "newspaper reporter." (In Mexico, I carried a press card that was never useful, not even for passing the security desk at the newspaper that issued the identification. Invariably, the vigilantes would call the editor to make sure I was the person I claimed to be. In the photo, I was ten years younger, undergoing the dynamic process of deformation by way of sleepless nights and drunken binges.) But this time I was finally able to stay at the scene of the crime without anyone bugging me. I had the luxury of exchanging my suspicions about the neighborhood's peculiarities with people who had lived their whole lives there. Almost all of my intelligence was untrue and based on commonalities to win over the trust of the other gossipers, all handpicked by me, and who were asking why someone would want to kill Leo the Homeless Man.

The police officers continued with their investigation, while the local residents took advantage of warning each other. I had seen, as if through a one-way mirror, the way they protected themselves from informers, a camera exposing this neighborhood in pain and always under suspicion. I had heard an unforgettable noise: a high-powered gun in action.

A miserable man had died due to flimsy motives in the same spot where I would regularly pass while on my way to get a haircut, buy vegetables at the market run by the Chinese, purchase alcohol, or eat tacos on Cypress Hill, known as a spot where drug dealers met. No one knew the victim or the assassin. To make things simple, one was Leo the Homeless Man, and the other was a twisted homie. That's what everyone said. A daily affair, and one wouldn't have to wait too long before someone else within the gears of crime would oil the clockwork of death.

As far as I was concerned, the case was closed. I was a partial witness to one of the frequent crimes in that part of the Bronx. Nothing mattered. From thereon, the homicide would become part of the statistical charts and tabula rasas onto which the barrio's personality was imprinted. Moreover, I doubted that the assassination would earn a spot on some corner of the *New York Post*. A black homeless man had died by the hands of an assassin well versed in the ever-increasing drive-by-shooting. He could have died from drugs, hypothermia, or cirrhosis. No one would claim the body; none of this interested anyone, apart from those long minutes in which the bloodied and deformed body, as if going through a rapid mummification, lay there waiting for the ambulance to come and take it away.

For me, death was like a frightening warning about that neighborhood immune to worry.

Leo had wandered around that area for many years, picking through trash or begging for blackened and gooey bananas from the store that the Caribbeans ran. His behavior was like that of other bums in other places: lost in his own thoughts and solitary. I would watch him often, and I failed at finding anything about his past or any details that would differentiate him from others like him. I never saw him eat, drink, or sleep. I never saw him stare at anyone or at anything in particular. While the paramedics rolled him into the ambulance and the police told everyone to keep on moving, I returned to the small talk that made daily life almost tolerable. Besieged by terror, racial strife, and obvious poverty, the apathetic crowd dispersed, each person jealously holding on to any clue that would make the cat-and-mouse game easier.

I returned to the store for my Colt 45 and I had no qualms about providing a detailed news report to the grocers. We made some guesses and jokes about the word on the street, and before I left the store, I had already forgotten about the touchy criticism made about Mexican boxers. My role as an informer was taken over by a scandalous pair of black men swigging their beers by the counter.

CHAPTER FIVE

In which...masturbation has a price (in Times Square)...
getting a job is easier than keeping one...Parrot will get
you a green card...the World Republic of Workers Who
Have No Papers...the Artist loves the Naked Empire.

Hot and bothered, she's pacing the room. All one can hear is the deafening sound track of "Green Onions" by Booker T. & the M.G.'s. She opens her thick lips and softly licks them. Then she struts to the bed, inviting me by crooking her index finger, urging me to follow her. She groans some words I can't make out, but I take them to mean "Hurry up." If I were able to unstick my gaze from her curves, the room would reach hyperrealist textures and dimensions. Moreover, I can smell her. Stretched out facedown, the blonde moves her hips, caressing them with the scarlet satin sheets. Someone's peering at her from the window. It's one of those muscular, meathead worker types. He sneaks inside, as if we weren't aware of his presence. She makes an over-rehearsed gesture of surprise upon seeing the intruder—one who's better endowed than myself, I guess. The only thing that bugs me is the warning that lets me know that my time is almost up. She smiles at me. She knows I'm not missing a detail. She turns her back to me as if to search for a small object among the folds of the sheets and then between her thighs, ready to proffer the final entrance to a shadowy and anonymous zone of *jouissance*. And that's how she remains: a sphinx in a leaf-storm awaiting the imminent TIME'S UP.

The intruder has taken advantage of the situation and he vigorously penetrates the woman, who takes it in without hesitation. They barely get undressed. What will follow will be a repetitive series of fade-ins, cuts, and close-ups of well-rounded and flexible flesh. The woman stretches out, ready, just like at the beginning, to receive the "unexpected" visitor for additional sessions. I remain there, a guest made of stone, observing this show of repetitions. The video footage doesn't jump despite the music that shakes the viewing booth: TIME'S UP.

Masturbation has a price. One token at a video booth gives you just one minute to reach your own money shot before an automatic curtain lowers down and blocks the monitor.

Pornography is pay-per-view. Pay just to see how we would like to view it all. Race doesn't matter as much as sizes and preferences. Times Square is governed by a special price: VIEW AND BE VIEWED.

$

Broadway, Eighth Avenue, and some neighboring streets still shelter the fading visages that once represented the sanctuaries of pornography. Like some show-off leaping up and down the stairs, through hallways and nooks, I realized just what one dollar could get you. It was the lowest package: four tokens and it let you watch videos in a tiny booth. This proved to be one of the cheapest, if not *the* cheapest, forms of entertainment in all of New York. Three minutes of unadulterated joy. You could pick a film from the digital screen, or by using the same tokens, despite the limitations in space and time, you could view some exotic dancer do a pole dance within a windowed polyhedron. This had a vague attraction to it. Depending on the willing nature of the dancer, and the urgent stares of the johns, the girl profited from the ever-increasing desperation of the johns that the automatic curtain would shortly descend: TIME'S UP...

...I had enough left over for my appointment on Fifty-Third Street with Parrot, a Salvadoran with eyes that looked like those of a hanged man. I was setting off with him to get some fake green cards that would let me land a job at an Italian restaurant called Remi on that very street where we met, at 145 West. Parrot was one of thousands of undocumented workers who never thought about when he was going to be slapped awake from the American Dream, but one who wished to stay on board the nightmare. He labored and sweated, mopping floors and scrubbing the grills in the kitchen where we met. He understood the edges between what was legal and illegal, and he behaved according to the years of experience reaped from time in his own country as well as this new one. At times he sold, rather than bought, his Salvi existentialisms. I liked his optimism and his faith, his proud allegiance to the World Republic of Workers Who Have No Papers.

My binge had started during the afternoon, downing beers in Chinatown while staring through the panorama of a Mexican dive. Canal Street seemed like it had been decorated by the owner of the Mexican dive. Then I headed toward SoHo, an area frequented by rich tourists and locals who have pretentions of belonging to the vanguard. The beggars didn't spook the spastic joy of the Benetton-type girls who drew out the *ahhs* and the *ohhs* of their imbecilic patter while they shopped for clothes that would show off the cutest ass. That trend of retro clothing had peaked among the pathological adolescents. The look that imitated black inmates proved to be the most popular. Some of them hid their well-rehearsed rage behind sunglasses that resembled those the Black Panthers had used. They showed off their brand-name jogging outfits and bling like they were OGs from the 1980s.

The white teenagers who had a watery and lysergic gaze belonged to many generations that had appropriated the style and slang of ancient slaves, and, moreover, they had become more and more adept at intimidating them. Those SoHo denizens would wait for midnight, and then they would wait for the call to set off to some warehouse rave where, with the help of amphetamines, they would let off some steam, all guided by the DJs. The decorative tackle that perforated their thin flesh looked like stigmas enslaving them to a fashion suited for their oily minds. Their addiction to that sugar and spacing out never impeded their ability to groove along to the rhythm of electronic and cybernetic music. Emergency Broadcast System Alert: New York finds itself flooded with what will shortly be the most serious health issue in the United States, diabetes and manic depression. The body language and garb of ravers, skaters, and rappers formed part of their pagan faith. Though they seemed free, secular, and libertine, they preached motley beliefs about the "great beyond."

For some reason or other, my soliloquy had become effusive. This was all due to my latest moves, which resulted in landing a job at an Italian restaurant. It was Monday at around eleven in the morning, and there I was, standing in line with around twenty other dudes in font of me in a kitchen corridor. At the end of the line there was a small office. We had to fill out some applications while we were interrogated. Latinos, all of us ...desperate...poised to lie about our experience, skills, and immigration status. We were ready to fish for any old shit job that would get the bills paid. I had the whim of writing down that I was a chef with years of experience, but I failed at convincing the lead chef, a Puerto Rican straight from the island, that I, a deliveryman, was suited for the position. He told me that the position had been filled "justa minute ago."

"We need people up here in the kitchen," he continued. "Yesterday, we hadda fire everyone. Are you in or out?"

Without giving me a second to think it over, he asked if I had my papers together. My response was enough to get me into the dressing room in order to start work at once. Right there and then, the Puerto Rican brought me an ID card with my name and then asked for me to double-check my entry code. It was 12:30 in the afternoon. Beside me, there were three other day laborers, thrilled about having found a mastah. Soon after that, I was wearing a chef's spotless white uniform, and I learned how to prep the salads from Arnulfo's instruction—he was from Puebla, Mexico—in a tiny station with barely enough room for two. Two hours later, the kitchen chef arrived and he called me into his office. He was a cynical and affected Italian who lisped perfect Castilian. And apart from being one of the two business partners, it made him feel like royalty to choose his own serfs.

"I want you to tell me the truth: Do you or do you not have a green card? Don't make me waste my time. The day before yesterday they took almost all of my kitchen workers. Immigration will come back before too long, and we don't want more problems or fines."

I stuck to my guns; my lie worked. The guy looked me in the eyes while he ordered me to inquire with the Puerto Rican when I should give him my documents.

I returned to the working life cursing myself for having missed the golden opportunity to be thrown out. I washed several pounds of lettuce, and for three hours they had me carrying boxes filled with fruits and vegetables from the refrigerator in the supply room to the railing where the same boxes where waiting, but now they were filled with scraps and waste, and I would dump them into some giant bins deep inside the kitchen. Then I reported to Arnulfo. His poor Spanish and his zeal to reveal the finer points about preparing each order confused me. He had been employed there for nine years, and he became one of the two or three trusted workers. His shift started at noon. I started asking questions about what had happened with *la migra*, and he didn't tell me much of anything. He preferred jabbering about the Mexican movies he would rent to watch late into the night. He instructed me with monosyllables, his chin pressed against his chest, his jaws always chewing a chunk of the tacos that were prepared during his shift. He would bring typical Mexican food that he kept in a cupboard beneath the railing, which he locked. It was his private cottage industry. By the middle of his shift, he would invite us to taste test his product, which was always well received, even by the Puerto Rican foreman. By that hour of my first shift, my nerves were already shot from the shouting, my clumsiness, the sauna-like heat, and my fear of slipping on the greasy floor or of burning myself when transporting heavy, boiling pots from one stovetop to another. I decided that I would get fired that very moment, so I spilled the beans: I had no papers. I was certain Arnulfo would run off immediately with the news.

"Hmm. Lemme talk with Papi. Let's see what he thinks."

He was referring to the Puerto Rican. He looked at me for a long while, leaving me on tenterhooks. We kept on working until there came a brief break, and that's when "Papi" approached us, as he was taking care of some business with one of the cooks. The Puerto Rican made himself understood by insulting everyone with a *madre* or a *papi* for any circumstance. He turned around in order to speak with Arnulfo, and he slapped his shoulders, so that they turned away from the earshot of the other cook. Upon returning to the station, Arnulfo said:

"No fuckin' problem. You can keep this gig. They'll figure out what to do while you're getting some papers; what you don't want is for them to boot you. How much they gonna pay you?"

"Six per hour, not including taxes. They won't pay for overtime for the first week."

"Holy shit! That's not bad. I'd even say you're lucky. I started out here earning three-fifty an hour."

He clicked his tongue while reading the orders as if they were litanies, and then he prepared four salad plates and four desserts. *You're here, so just fuckin' deal with it,* I said to myself. I had no more good excuses for abandoning a steady paycheck.

Arnulfo bugged me no end. He ate his words; he drooled and hummed songs while piling up the plates for me, one after the other, as according to the orders of the Puerto Rican, who never took his eyes off me and who shouted, "Hurry up, Papi!" I was in a daze, and I was scared of making the slightest mistake, even though I tried to convince myself I had nothing to lose. I did the best I could, but I wasted desserts that the *poblano* remade. A little after one in the morning, they stopped serving. Now I had to clean and organize everything except for the floor and the grills.

The cooks glanced at me askance, yet they didn't ask me where I was from. There were twenty of us in that subterranean hall where, even though the stoves were turned off, we sweated profusely. The Puerto Rican was the first one to leave after the chef. When it came to be my turn to change by the filthy lockers stinking of feet and sweat, almost everyone else had left. There were only four others left behind, equally mistrustful of me. They talked among themselves, ignoring me. I learned that they too didn't have their work permits. In a friendly manner, I began to inquire just how one would start the process of getting one's hands on some paper, and they understood what I meant at once. Finally, another *poblano* informed me that they were waiting for Parrot, who worked during the early-morning hours. He could get his hands on false documents for some dough.

"How much?"

"Don't know. You gotta talk that over with him."

Parrot showed up whistling and cracking vulgar jokes about everyone. While he changed, the others formed a small group around him.

"What? All y'all need your fake papers? I need some photos. Right here, on Fifth and Forty-Third, they'll take them for fifteen dollars. Bring 'em to me tomorrow, and I'll get your stuff ready by the next day."

One of them already had his package ready. Silently, as if they were selling drugs on the corner, he gave Parrot a thin roll of bills and the photos. Then he quickly left, happy and saying good-bye. He even forgot his winter cap with the Lakers logo.

"How much will it be?" I immediately asked.

"One-twenty."

"Why not a hundred?"

"Why not one-fifty?"

"Hold on, I'm not even the chef."

"Damn, you wish. The biz isn't mine. I'm just helpin' out a buddy. It's a good price. If you don't believe me, go ask around on Forty-Second Street."

No one else haggled with Parrot, and I didn't know what to do about getting some false papers down on Forty-Second Street. In a few seconds, I made an evaluation of my physical state, of the possibilities of getting a less demanding job and that that Parrot-eyed Salvadoran, who jittered and hustled, would try to rip me off.

"What time do I see you?" I said at last.

"Today, my Prince Charming. Ten minutes before the afternoon shift starts."

"It's a deal."

The Parrot came to an agreement with everyone there, and then he went to work.

$

My appreciation for the areas surrounding Lexington and Grand Central had not changed since the day I landed in New York, months prior. I searched for the best place to take the photos. I had become more careful when it came to my interactions with fellow countrymen and day laborers. But the gringos' indifference to us was apparent. The magnificent architecture and the functional luxury left spaces perfect for losing oneself among the chaos of pedestrians and vehicles, the begging on street corners, and the rank blizzards stinking of the sea and diesel.

I entered one of the few photo shops that didn't sell apocryphal identifications. I was helped by a clerk who seemed to be Hindu. His disdain when it came to charging me the fifteen dollars, which he demanded before handing over two photos the size for a driver's license, stank of Mexico's culture of coyotes and petty bureaucrats. That posturing of one who feels empowered by having under his control one of the threads in some racket. That's what downtown was like at noon: everything was permitted, everyone could do what he damn well pleased, as long as the cash register was ringing.

I reached the restaurant ten minutes prior to my starting time at four. Parrot was already waiting for me, surrounded by the three other cooks, in order to check out the quality of their photos. I wasn't going to fork over a cent until he handed me my fake papers. Parrot was in a hurry; he had shown up only in order to seal some deals. He glanced at the photos and then clucked his tongue and looked at me, completely dumbfounded.

"It slipped my mind to tell you that they shouldn't be frontal shots, but from the side. What you got here is for driver's licenses."

While I swallowed my frustration, the other workers began to loosen up and feel happy and self-confident about having successfully passed the first step in this process. From within the office, the Puerto Rican was still hiring. He then stepped out, walking through the kitchen and locker room, asking who had papers. He received more nos than yeses. Those who had been working there for a while cussed at him as soon as he turned his back.

"And so what do we do now?" I asked, my mouth gone dry.

"Well, my Prince Charming, ya gotta get them taken again, and we'll meet tomorrow, but at dawn, at three thirty, before I start my shift, because today I'm not punching in; it's my day off."

"What? Can't I go where you get the papers?"

"You must be crazy. I'll wait for you on Fifty-Third and Sixth, right by the statue."

"Fine."

All day I was in a bad mood, indifferent to the Puerto Rican's shouting and Arnulfo's instructions. I would also have the next day off according to my schedule.

That's why I was loafing around Avenue of the Americas while a soft drizzle slowly disappeared toward the north of the island. The cars seemed to circle by on an electric walkway delineated by buildings and shop windows, and the crowds concealed drug trafficking among stalls selling knickknacks. Beyond the mist to the north, the night sparkled like a theater marquee in the middle of nowhere.

Leaving work at the end of the evening, I was struck by the urge to get a tattoo. I predicted that in Chinatown or the East Village I would find a parlor with low prices. Moreover, the wait until dawn to meet up with Parrot would become less tedious. I took a walk through Saint Mark's Place to pick up flyers advertising tattoo parlors. They all claimed to be the oldest and the best in the city. I visited them and found out that they were either closed or packed with clients. They looked like barber shops, but with skyrocket prices. In one of the places—filled with punks waiting their turns—the patter of two girls in charge of piercings and the wait list poked fun at the affected and outlandish attire of the clients. Everyone was a neophyte itching to appear on the cover of one of those glossy magazines dictating the counterculture's fashion sense.

One of the girls quoted the price of a tattoo that I had chosen from the catalog. Upon seeing me pause pensively, she muttered in horrible Spanish, *"Doscientos dólares,"* while making a V with her fingers. I laughed in her face and told her to take a shower in Spanish before turning around, the bovine-like gazes of the punks following me as I exited. No longer wanting that particular tat, I bar-hopped all the way to a cheaper tattoo parlor in Chinatown, but I realized I no longer had enough money. I preferred to spend my cash on a flask of liquor and make my way tranquilly toward Forty-Second Street and Eighth Avenue.

$

Times Square was a place of polarities, concepts regarding good and evil, what was plain or sophisticated. All carried an artificial licentiousness. I was able to be a witness to its puritanical retrogression. Its warm decadence was demolished to make room for a moral architecture financed by Disney, among other conglomerates. Forty-Second Street maintained its appearance of being a phantasmal port with stranded auditoriums waiting to be rescued. Financially infeasible, and without an eager public, they remained lobbies and marquees, like works of art brut whose aphorisms and minimalist flyers meant nothing to the pedestrians attentive to the constant beat of crime or some show of force by the police stationed in that section.

Bogged down by the impossibility to fabricate new desires, the pornography in Times Square repeated itself in an incessant tautology, which exasperated the solitary person until he exploded. Some of the peep shops operated fourteen hours a day, 365 days a year. Within those live pay-per-views, everyone played the role of each other's sentinel.

The Naked Empire offered a good number of booths that featured shows for the individual in exchange for a token running the price of five bucks. The client, kept at a distance by a virtual and a real window, would haggle over the "remuneration" for his well-rehearsed fantasy, with twenty dollars as a bare minimum. By the door to the booths, the women took turns dancing within the great central polyhedron with faint multicolor lighting. The gawkers looked alike, placed within a multiple confession booth. Hands in pockets, they did their best to reel in their obvious hard-ons before the automatic curtain lowered when the time was up, forcing them to wander off like lost souls in search of eye candy in the building to prolong their peeping, even without the possibility of a money shot.

The Naked Empire was the most popular porno dome and my favorite as well. Its prestige won coverage in the *New York Times*, and yet its prices were within reach. It was located on the corner of Port Authority, a bus terminal whose surroundings and atmosphere were reminiscent of the San Lázaro terminal in Mexico City. Another one of the attractions at the Naked Empire was its setting and dynamics, which heralded the freak shows of time past. Those circuses of the grotesque, those mirrors of morbidity, with the credulity in good and evil, would put on live shows that showcased genetic disorders, anthropologic exoticisms, and freaks of nature. The principal attractions always fell into the categories of women who were tattooed, bearded, or Siamese. In the Naked Empire there were also women covered with fur or suffering from other cases when genetics spin out of control. There was also a small store with magazines and all types of accessories, which would let someone, feigning disinterest, be introduced to the Disneyland of stuffed toys. The place's layout used the spatial and philosophic principles of Jeremy Bentham, an English economist who, during the utilitarianism of the eighteenth century, designed a blueprint that, though never put into practice according to its original purpose, was apt for hospitals, factories, schools, and prisons. The project consisted of a concentric building; in the middle there would be an observation tower that could control each cell or room, but the disadvantage of the observed was he would never know if he was being watched. As a representative of political liberalism, Bentham proposed this idea as based on the principle of utilitarianism: the greatest happiness for the greatest number. Amen.

The Naked Empire was a panopticon where not even in the most isolated booth could one achieve absolute anonymity. All in all, it offered four entrances and exits to the street, maintaining a dubious discretion that ultimately interested no one.

Times Square breathed a tacky and harsh aesthetic reminiscent of the 1970s. Funk, soul, and disco were the customary sound tracks to lasciviousness and grinding hips. Attire, decor, and atmosphere were scenes of erotic fantasies from a mind burning with a Saturday night fever.

The United States has been cautious about not merely cranking out the inherent monotony in its messianic productivity. The attractiveness of myths buttressed by consumerism loses its charm when it's marked down or not in demand. America's madness to invent the dispensable and then recycle it, its talent for novelty and self-parody, hides the phobias of a nation fleeing in full haste from boredom. An adolescent.

For me, New York City was like a kingdom without a unifying sermon, one where "minority" races and sexual orientations, the sick and the deformed, the homeless and the pariahs, each in his own way, all contributed to maintain that market of deliriums. It was a city that, despite its intense amount of street traffic, was invaded by heartless pedestrians whose dreams were nourished by the vertigo of the present instant.

$

And it came to pass that there was a Better Business Bureau in charge of cleaning up Times Square. Starting in 1992, those notable individuals commenced scrubbing their kingdom of carnal sin, a kingdom of fifty-nine apples, so that they may continue to bleed—I mean, attract—at least twenty million visitors per year. The feudal lords decided to each contribute a portion of his riches, taking precautions to hide the amounts. Thus that zone of circus and acrobatics, theater, and catwalks reaped the benefits from the generosity of those noblemen. An edict available for viewing in tourist information centers proclaimed that thirty-nine individuals dressed as peasants would collaborate with the police to watch over the feudal streets for fifteen hours each day, which made me assume that during the remaining nine hours everything would return to normal.

The muggings, rapes, drug trafficking, and murders had given Manhattan its fame as a city of psychotic stratum and a mecca of yellow journalism, those tabloids with stories like the one about the two exotic dancers who were dismembered shortly before the royal campaign for beautification commenced. Two admirers who were upset about being rejected by the strippers divided them between themselves by slicing them up with hunting knives purchased at a specialty shop for police paraphernalia next to Naked Empire. Despite the fact that the homicides didn't occur in Times Square, the girls worked in the Porno-dome, and the report in the *Daily News* did little to avoid feeding the black legend of streets invaded by thousands of tourists in search of a "Travis," the Taxi Driver who would take them for a spin.

Pornography in Times Square was so ubiquitous that not mentioning it wasn't as if you didn't notice it. In pairs, plainclothesmen kept watch on the corners between Forty-First and Fifty-Third Streets, from south to north, and from Eight Avenue to the Avenue of the Americas, from west to east. The taciturn uniformed officers, always hoping for some ruckus that would make them the stars of video cameras and flashbulbs, tolerated the sale of drugs and panhandling to the rhythm of rap while the Asian procurers dragged pedestrians into sex shops.

The zone gathered together businesses and services, including gyms, boutiques, massage parlors, theaters playing films from the "straight-to-video" industry (which, in Hollywood, is code for porn), even lectures on the sex industry and its intense activity. For a while, I was an assiduous scholar of *Screw*, a humorous tabloid filled with gossip about the porno scene, parodies, and photomontages of politicians and starlets of that particular world of theater. Pornography floated in a swamp of appetites through which thousands of rowers navigated blindly. Despite all that, the market for street sex was disappearing slowly, incapable of competing with hotlines, the Internet, massage parlors, and escort agencies. Sexual satisfaction delivered to your door won over adept clients at a dizzying pace; it was a service in which the quality of the service provided, and the indifference about it, became more palatable. The new aphrodisiac for the alienated is fiber optics.

$

The part of Naked Empire reserved for the consumption of alcoholic beverages was decorated as an event hall. "Lessy" chose me, and she sat in my lap. She probably came to this agreement as a result of never having listened to her parents. She confessed to earning roughly $300 on a good day, after a shift of ten hours that left her with ragged feet from repeating her routine over and over and over again. I made her feel better by letting her know how much I earned in a restaurant after an equally long shift. She erupted in laughter, revealing the golden bridge near her right incisors. Her conversation was coarse despite the finesse with which she tried to rub her pendant breasts against me. I spent time with her because my drunkenness took over me, yet without the elemental pleasure demanding that I get horny from the available offer. When Lessy figured out that my satisfaction resided only in drinking more beer, she returned to the dais to finish her turn. For a buck, she would show her cunt, almost permitting me to reveal it when I unfolded a dollar into her black G-string. A buck can get a smile to express any desire. As for me, it reminded me that I needed at least three more to order a whiskey. A group of Japanese men observed us; one of them raised his beer in order to make a toast with us. His smile was a cyclopean slit on a face bathed in blue light.

Lessy got down from the red-carpeted dais in order to go with the Japanese men. My beer tasted like mineral water. I had no interest in any of the other dancers. They moved their asses with no style, with no drive to exude grace, because they simply had none, no matter how hard they tried. The demand there—which wasn't great—was driven by the Asian crowd, who suffered because they also looked after their luggage filled with cameras and other apparatuses. They didn't stop smiling at the dancers. Despite their resistance to the onslaught of G-strings and garter belts, they left a few dollars under the elastic straps before running from the hall with the puerile gestures of neophytes in nocturnal adventures. Lessy returned to my table to wish me luck and she gave me a card with the address of another place where she worked, in TriBeCa, by the Franklin subway stop. I would have forgotten about Lessy had it not been for a girlfriend, a year later, who asked me to take her to a burlesque and we went to the infamous place where Lessy, on a Saturday at four in the afternoon, was eating her lunch of Kentucky Fried Chicken, sprawled out on a divan by the foot of a stage. Other strippers were eating hamburgers, going around, here and there, to go up and do their number. Others, astride cushioned chairs, sought to reanimate the septuagenarian seated beneath them for forty bucks. The chairs looked electric beneath the red lights.

I finished my drink. I was about to get up and find Parrot when James Brown hollered from the depths of his ancestral hell, "This is a man's world!"

I asked for one for the road to raise my glass to the Godfather.

$

Outside, a place with a capacity for perhaps thirty seats. They announced the best live variety show where, for fifteen bucks, they promised oral sex, anal sex, and hot scenes of love from Lesbos. The show lasted—though this was not on the ticket—for fifteen minutes. The prolonged pauses between one act and another were filled up with videos, their volumes blasting, from two enormous screens facing each other. Fleeting trails of dust specks filtered through the vaudevillian lighting, which animated the harsh, sudden appearance of two strippers clacking their red-and-black patent leather high-heeled boots. One of the two, the aggressive blond one, placed a small black briefcase atop one of the tables. The other one, darker in complexion, waited among the seats with a vacant gaze. The blonde made her role clear by taking out different objects and showing them to the public. They were all available at the bazaar in the Naked Empire.

The show started off with vaginal penetration by way of a humongous pink vibrator that then died, yet we sensed this would result in a coitus interruptus, obliging an intermediary to carry on with the act, while one of the performers retrieved an alkaline rabbit that hadn't run out of its juice. But the blonde just began to dance as if she were within the polyhedron, peepholes surrounding her. She continued grinding her hips, bored, until the darker one returned to the platform after a few minutes, armed with new batteries, in order to load the only vibrating thing in that performance space, which reminded one of the machine in *A Clockwork Orange*, where Little Alex is put through the expiation test.

"The show must go on!" demanded one of the more anxious audience members. The couple then moved with dexterity despite their platform boots and nine-inch heels. They performed in a perfunctory way, like clowns at family parties where everyone knows the usual tricks and gags. Among the scattered attendants, there were three old men with moldy expressions on their faces from having spent years viewing the scene from the second row. A couple of black women, much more attractive as well as younger than the show's starlets, challenged the timorous crowd gathered in the seats, and they took on the dare to stick a flashlight near the vaginas spreading on the platform. Some guy behind me looked on without paying attention; he was just checking how much time remained before returning to his spot programing the music and videos. The ecstatic black chicks screamed obscenities at the two who seemed to be celebrating a silver wedding anniversary with vibrators, whips, and jelly, all to the rhythm of go-go.

Another old man, entombed in his corner seat, rose from his crypt and pulled out a five-spot from his pocket for the darker stripper and got entangled in the duel. He took the vibrator; he first made it disappear between her ass cheeks, inserting it in her anus, and he invited the blonde to extract it with her teeth. Finally, throwing kisses and putting things back in the briefcase, they exited the stage, hand in hand. Once their asses were devoured by the penumbra of the exit, those in the auditorium, once again, turned their eyes to the screens, awaiting the next floor show.

$

Times Square was for riffraff and Greenwich Village, along with SoHo, was reserved for New York's bohemians. On Sixth Avenue there were two twin movie joints showing XXX films twenty-four hours a day. What was really hard-core had nothing to do with the marathon of porn, but with the faces that recognized each other in the light of the projector. Bodily humors rubbing themselves against the plastic seats provided some personality to the general mistrust. The current spectators gave us their shoulders despite the fact that voluntary overcrowding came with groping and sex traffic. Whenever it came to a possible hookup, what always proved difficult was slinking from the grotesqueness. That's where the subsistence of New York resided: spaces reserved for any mercantile interest. That's when I opened my perception to a world that considered itself "cosmopolitan."

It was an anonymous meeting taking place among some guys trying to ejaculate in a group while watching the images flickering on the screen. That was the weirdest element. The rest were just jacking off to literature.

Modesty ceases when mystery no longer exists. Pornography lacks a discourse, something obvious. Trying to come to terms with this seemed futile to me. I was already a peeping Tom, so none of it had much to offer me. Cunnilingus, fellatio, sodomy, masturbation, sadism, groans, moans, seeking out, solitude, escape, exasperation—who gives a fuck? I was looking for something else, perhaps a bit base and burlesque, but capable of weaving its way through irreverence, scandal, and transgression. Part of my morbid hedonism served to dull the pain and frustration of working as a day laborer.

Times Square was a symbol of segregation. The unproductive maelstrom no longer had a place in the inoffensive peep shops. Times Square agonized as an oratory for solitary beings. There, at the end of the day, love would continue being unreachable, like absolute virtue.

If pornography is a moral sickness, it is still healthy enough to earn the respect that comes from being magnificent.

$

I arrived ten minutes late to my appointment. I was nervous that ol' Parrot-Eye had left already. I had the whim that I should walk toward the restaurant and, hiding behind a marble pillar, spy and see the kitchen staff leave. As always, they rushed toward the subway. Through the big glass doors, I could make out the girl who worked the cash register speaking to one of the waiters. He was a gringo and part of the staff, and, like the rest of them, he always tried to be polite with the "people in the kitchen." A Mexican busboy exited from the place, short and nervous—that one, yep, he had papers that were legit, and who knows what he had to do to get them. He told me that Parrot hadn't been in all day. He knew why I was looking for him but said nothing, and stiffly, but politely, said good-bye, wishing me good luck. I returned to Fifty-Third and Sixth and I smoked a couple of cigarettes before I saw Parrot turn around the corner that I had been spotting for a long while. He walked as if he were being pushed onto the scene. I almost applauded him before giving him my photos.

"These'll work. Tomorrow I'll give you the papers. I'll give them to you at night in the restaurant."

I nodded my head, relieved at getting that off my chest. My displeasure at working there changed as a result of having done something that would help me in the future. Parrot spoke to me of his activities during the day; they all involved money, but not a lot, and nothing interesting. He had his finger in every pot: positions that needed to be filled, cuttin' corners, and problems between workers I didn't know. The drinks made me boring and somnolent. I was starting to feel the consequences of my drinking binge, and a hangover was looming ahead. All I wanted was to crash into my sheets and to never think about anything ever again. Parrot didn't say a thing about my dragon breath. He watched me with his speculating gaze, trying to size me up and see if I knew more than what I feigned. And then I thought of asking him:

"Bring me where they make the fake ones. I want to see how they're printed."

"You must be crazy, my handsome prince. It ain't my biz. I already told you I just help my buddy and I don't know how he gets the numbers and printed stuff."

That sufficed. I was beginning to grow cold and feeling anxious about getting home after such a night. I said good-bye, and from the middle of the street, I glanced back and saw Parrot take off in great strides, as if he were hiding from someone, although no one was nearby.

CHAPTER SIX

Dispatch from New York City:
The Terrible Fate of Monika Beerle, Aspiring Ballerina

Saint Gallen, in the northeast of Switzerland, was shook from its alpine tranquillity because of an article printed by a newspaper with one of the largest distributions in the world: the *New Zurich News*, or NZN. A young woman had unwillingly become a publicist for the town. That very night, the local news spread the image of an ambitious girl who had left for the United States in search of fame and fortune. The scandalous news item was treated in a manner reserved for exceptional events. However, neither the images nor the pedantic tone of the anchorman, even on mute, was what the inhabitants of Saint Gallen—famous for its embroidery— would hope for as a source of pride. The remains of Monika Beerle, twenty-six years old, had been discovered in a plastic container in a New York bus station.

"Oh my Lord, Monika, this can't be so!" was what her father, Soren Beerle, prostrate with grief, was able to muster in front of the television camera, incapable of finishing an embroidered apron with his wife that they were going to send to their daughter. Mrs. Beerle received the news as if she were being knocked on the head and as if each blow was increasing in intensity. Her first reaction was to keep the phone off the hook to avoid taking any unwanted calls and to help her husband, who suffered from asthma.

The terrifying confirmation of the event was the culmination of his many warnings to his daughter to not leave the dreary routine of Saint Gallen without a husband, the city being a famous destination for some of the richest men in Europe.

$

In Grand Central train station, a few blocks from the scene of the crime, an elegantly attired suspect was seated on the stairs that led to Vanderbilt Avenue. His gaze, protected behind dark glasses, glanced alternately between the hundreds of pedestrians on their way to the subway, the tunnels accessing out-of-town trains, and his copy of the *New York Post*. The headline spoke of the homicide with a gruesome photo that confirmed New York's reputation. Calmly, the suspect approached one of the ticket windows. He bought a train ticket. It was the last time Randy Easterday would see that city for a long, long time.

$

Monika Beerle, an aspiring ballerina, left Saint Gallen with more enthusiasm than money, bent on finding her fortune in America, no matter what the price. In the spring of 1988, she reached the place of her dreams: New York City. Monika immediately sought a job that would allow her to live well and cover her ballet studies. The world's largest job market didn't hesitate in presenting options to that Aryan beauty. Reluctant about accepting any more jobs as a nanny, which kept her indoors and the victim of bratty children and arrogant parents, and after eight months of living in Manhattan, she decided to work at a topless bar. The proposal came from a Polish woman who had worked as a nanny; Monika met her while strolling down the tree-lined walkway of Riverside Drive on the Upper West Side, one of the more exclusive neighborhoods on the Hudson. The offer came with a lot of money and the excitement of entering a different world, and she would remain anonymous, avoiding becoming the target of judgments and critiques on the part of her family and her hometown. Monika made an appointment to be introduced to the manager of the bar, in Times Square, and the next day she made her debut as "Sussie" before the restrained applause of the scattered clientele of office workers, tourists, and retirees.

Neither the pay nor the atmosphere was ideal. Sussie wanted more. The recognition and few dollars she received didn't match her dreams of success.

That dingy atmosphere of fake, discreet elegance made her cautious; however, a man by the name of Daniel Rakowitz began to get her attention. A frequent client, he would spend hours observing her from the closest tables or from the velvet chairs in the rooms for private shows. He was tall and corpulent. He always dressed impeccably in suit and tie. He would light a Benson & Hedges and let it smolder in the ashtray without taking a single drag. He would rarely finish his goblet of red wine. At times he would walk out of the place, leaving only smoke and a half-finished pack of cigarettes. He often asked why such a beautiful being would hide itself in the dark, stripping to the beat of disco.

By force of habit, they became friends; they would look at each other and exchange wide smiles whenever Rakowitz would place a twenty-dollar bill in Sussie's G-string. After all, the management wouldn't tolerate any discourtesy to someone who regularly spent around $100 on admission, drinks, and tips for the dancers. Rakowitz seemed financially solvent and refined; he politely rejected Sussie's offers to give him a lap dance at his table. He seemed to be there as the mere result of being a solitary person. Because of that, after a few weeks or perhaps months, he invited her on a date, and Sussie, despite the rule prohibiting those types of agreements at the workplace, took the time to call the number that was printed in elegant calligraphy on a piece of a cigarette box, which she found folded inside a twenty-dollar bill that Rakowitz slipped into her G-string on his last visit to Hot Lips. Rakowitz's company, full of metaphors and dollars, became an option for her, something different from the tremulous specters and sweaty flesh that kept her away from her goals. Months later, they were sharing an apartment in the East Village. Dan Rakowitz never demanded a thing from her, apart from faith in the Supreme Being.

Monika worked hard. She slept in late, and during her free time, she worked out in one of the bedrooms reserved for this. Her dosage of cocaine was increasing slowly. She had found a bag of five grams "by accident" in Rakowitz's chest of drawers. She never asked why he kept it where it was easy to come across nor why he had it. Despite the fact that she would inhale a bit each day, Rakowitz never got upset about the shrinking amount in his stash.

As the weeks and months sped by, Monika's choreography was an uninterrupted dream sating the fantasies of lonely men.

Rakowitz rarely left the apartment. He was a recluse who never hesitated to avoid others; he considered them to be "perverse and ignorant." "Don't you see your graces wither in the mirrors before you?" "The old triumphs of evil of which you consider yourself an expert...do you not back away in stiff horror, when Nature has made you into hated genius?" Rakowitz would repeat those questions, memorized from an old edition of Baudelaire's works, to Monika with decreasing sweetness. He never greeted his neighbors, and no one ever saw him buying anything in any of the neighborhood stores. When Rakowitz was around, music wasn't permitted and the television was turned off. The only possible distraction for him and, as a result, for Monika was reading from the Book of Mormon and passages of Baudelaire. Slowly, Rakowitz unfolded his personality. He showed complete indifference to the outside world and for Monika's caresses; he observed her in leaden silence. Whenever he felt annoyed, he would shout at Monika and scold her for not memorizing psalms and verses. However, he never prohibited her livelihood as a stripper, and sometimes he would sweetly ask her to dance naked to "Angel Face," the piece Monika used during her routine, while he watched her leaning against the window frame in the bedroom. Monika knew nothing about him: she didn't know his friends, what his past was like, or what places he would frequent, apart from a church in the East Village surrounded by buildings filled with Puerto Ricans, punks, proletarian bohemians imitating the Beats and Amiri Baraka, heroin addicts, and after-hours clubs. His medical insurance card said that he was originally from Texas.

On the night of August 29, 1989, Rakowitz returned to the apartment. He had locked Monika inside. He had also disconnected the telephone, thrown away the mail, and, without Monika's knowledge, told her parents several weeks earlier while she was working that she had moved to California with a friend, leaving no address.

Both were in a state of nervous breakdown, but Rakowitz's state was almost epileptic. He would mutter incomprehensible sentences, and he accused her of being irredeemable. His gaze never moved from his "flower of evil." They argued. There was shouting, insults, and a disgusted smirk from the ballerina whenever Rakowitz tried to grab her while spitting lines from "Une Charogne" and passages from the Bible. She tried to flee and, as a response, Rakowitz hit her repeatedly with a pipe covered with paper and tape, embedded a new candle into her anus, and then fell unconscious and exhausted on the carpet. Used to hearing arguments through the walls, neighbors ignored the quarrel by turning up their televisions. Seventy-two hours later, the dismembered body of Monika Beerle, better known as Sussie, was found in one of the baggage lockers at Penn Station.

The detectives' investigation wove a connection to satanic rituals. However, apart from data taken from a witness, who provided them with the features of two suspects who had used the lockers, the investigation became mired in redundant information, with no way of finding the suspects.

The weeks that followed the homicide swarmed with news in the morning and evening tabloids and on episodes of *True Crimes*, whose producers were already fed up with summarizing crimes caused by urban crowding and poverty, and the gossip and intrigues of famous athletes and entertainment figures. The conjectures couldn't wait, and the death of Monika was linked to an international prostitution ring, and it also helped Mayor Dinkins in his campaign against the sex trade in Times Square. The press couldn't resist summoning the presence of a new "Son of Sam," that serial killer who rattled the city's nerves during a summer seventeen years prior.

For three years, the matter was considered "under investigation." It wasn't until February 14, 1992, midafternoon, when Lieutenant Robert Nardoza, the son of Dominican immigrants, received a long-distance call in his cubicle from Easton, Pennsylvania.

"We arrested Randy Easterday."

"Where?"

"In a library. He didn't resist. He only asked for some time to change his contact lenses for glasses."

"Good. Keep me in the loop."

After hanging up the phone, he looked through his files for the one on Monika "Sussie" Beerle. He found a photo of her, one that her parents had sent. She was smiling and holding some skies. He set it atop his coffee mug on the desk while he looked over the file and took some deep puffs from a menthol cigarette. He wrote on his agenda: "Randy Easterday, suspect for homicide and tampering with evidence."

From the start of the investigation, the agents had tried to tie together various sects rumored to practice satanic rituals. One of the clues was the receipt from a library loan in the urn of one of the churches that they were staking out. It was made out to Randy Easterday, an addict who covered up his paranoid personality with the image of being a lover of literature and whose features matched those provided by the bus terminal employee. Easterday would recruit initiates to his sect from libraries and rehabs. Some of them disappeared when they found out there was someone asking for their whereabouts.

Lieutenant Nardoza immediately filed an extradition order to New York, where after long interrogations and visits to the judge, the state court jailed Easterday with a verdict in sight that teetered between life imprisonment and the psychiatric ward. In his confessions, full of contradictions, there appeared Dan Rakowitz, his lover and one of the leaders in the sect in which they both participated. A year before that, Rakowitz had been pegged as the main suspect in the ballerina's murder, but he was set free upon determining him mentally unsound. Rakowitz shortly disappeared thereafter, but police didn't lose trace of him.

The capture of the litterateur had helped police gain valuable information, leading them to the Church of the Realized Fantasy in the East Village. Members of the sect there were captured during a ceremony that included human sacrifice and the ingestion of blood and hallucinogens. Rakowitz was picked up in the raid; he was naked, thinner by several pounds, and in a state of ecstasy. The fourteenth of

February...an ironic date to trap someone linked to a fanatical homicide.

Nardoza declared to the press that Rakowitz remained the prime suspect. His ties to the death of Monika Beerle could not be denied, though he remained silent. A year later, the psychopath appealed and he was subjected to clinical tests. His testimony, along with evidence found in the East Village apartment, which also included a diary belonging to Rakowitz in which he inserted "Sussie" into verses by Baudelaire, confirmed him as the perpetrator of three additional murders, as well as being a drug trafficker. All the while, Rakowitz remained calm, convinced that his crimes were part of a divine undertaking, greedy for impious blood and order. With the same calmness, on February 22, 1992, he accepted his sentence to life imprisonment in a psychiatric facility. There were two spots that were always empty in the courtroom: those belonging to Monika's parents, as they considered their presence to be useless once the remains of Monika had been returned to Saint Gallen. They politely received the media prying into their lives. They proudly showed off their alpine cabin and family album. Moreover, they participated on a reality show; Mrs. Beerle didn't tire of weeping while she spoke before a live audience of fond family memories involving her daughter, all dubbed by an aspiring local actress. After having his sentence read to him, Rakowitz poeticized the moment in court: "I envy the lowest beasts who can fall into a stupid sleep while the skein of time slowly unwinds."

On his way home the day following Rakowitz's sentencing, Lieutenant Nardoza was immersed in the data and routine numbers involving crime. He thought about investigation techniques and prevention, as well as the answers he had to give to a sensationalist press. He recalled the heated report delivered by the Senate committee, which concluded that crime was increasing due to the easy acquisition of weapons, drug trafficking, and demographic growth. "Shit, everyone knows that. And I don't get paid a fortune, unlike those good-for-nothings."

Then he stopped in front of a newsstand, and he bought a *Sports Illustrated* and the evening edition of the *Post*. On the tabloid's last page, there was a montage of Times Square and an image of his face as well as Rakowitz's, both hanging in the balance of Lady Justice wearing Monika's face. He smiled with satisfaction, knowing full well that a part of his job consisted of filling up a theater where there were seats for everyone. He lit a cigarette after refusing to give some spare change to an old woman who blessed him nonetheless, and he thought about the three kinds of faith: in Fame, in God, and in Justice. After all, he concluded, they have more in common than it seems.

CHAPTER SEVEN

In which...the Artist considers the plight of the inexhaustible worker...the day laborer's addiction to the dollar is retold...the drug of exhaustion overcomes the Artist.

The average wage for undocumented workers was six dollars an hour. With a Social Security card, even if it was fake, nobody could avoid paying taxes, unless they paid you under the table. I asked questions of other day laborers, who were often hostile or suspicious, as to how they got hired. Almost all of them were recommended by a family member or someone from their hometown. Those with the most experience said that after two years of work, things would improve. The trick was to grin and bear it. Bosses liked inexhaustible workers who kept their mouths shut. No one would investigate anyone else's experience because they were all identical. And for each poor soul who had a tragedy to share, there was someone else with an even more gruesome Calvary. I lived surrounded by tough types, in a religious sense: Jesuit-like, ready for the most absurd sacrifices as long as they could get a pot to piss in.

In reality, I was correct to doubt myself. I came from a monstrous city that carried a black legend and that many of the workers had experienced in the flesh while they attempted to find a job there. My origin was evident in the way I walked and talked, in the way I interacted with others, often against my own will, and this offended them. I had no reservations about cursing the Mexican government and Mexicans. I would walk down 125th Street in Harlem, around the Apollo, convinced that James Brown was a musical genius. Single, I would get drunk during the workweek, and I never spoke of my plans to bring my family to the United States. Quite the contrary...I had managed to hook up with women in similar circumstances. I met almost all of them in English class or by way of Rose. None of them knew each other, and they were ready to receive me in their homes and tend to me as if I were the only man on the face of the earth, just as long as I would listen to them and not make them feel as if they were idiots. I had learned that almost all of them had been made to feel like imbeciles, and that was the cause of their divorces, loneliness, grudges, and fear. They hopped from one man to another between long stretches of abstinence, as if they were trying to piece together a single lover. For some reason, those women were attracted to taking care of someone, as if their frustrations needed to make a payment. In the beginning, they were attracted to the high-and-mighty type who relies on the old trick of saying, "Tell me about your problems and I will take care of them." It still works as an aphrodisiac for both parties. Those who succeed in escaping from the chastity belt give in to an enormous sexual appetite, feeling safe and trustful, and without any regrets. In the end, they're all alike. Those are my type of women. All in all, I was what I appeared to be: an unbeliever in permanent emotional bankruptcy...just like them.

Up till then, my money had been spent on English courses, room and board, and some other much-needed distractions. By paying attention to advice on how to "get ahead in life," I would spend all of my savings within a few years, trying to cure my ailments caused by working short stints. The exhaustion started within me, but it soon became visible. For day laborers it's like steam from a boiler about to explode: his tubes, valves, muscles, and calluses being worn away become visible in his yellowed eyes and the waxen shade of his skin, manifest in gastric ulcers and premature ailments. The foremen pretended to encourage us in order to cover up their abuses and intimidation, and they feigned a blind confidence in their workers who supposedly benefitted from the altruism of an hourly wage.

I had no need to connect with those machines greased with fatalism, poverty, and evil Uncle Sam. Besides, they already had their place as legionnaires of social justice and a new racial identity, although they were the first to turn a cold shoulder to a new arrival ready to break his back working alongside them. Those tools of contraband provided endless material for politicians, professors, well-intentioned reporters who knew little or nothing at all about the motives and worldview of the day laborer.

On both sides of the border, the discourse chose extremism as a point of view: suffering, death by hyperthermia, sunstroke, or drowning in deserts and rivers; coyotes, bloodthirsty border patrol agents, humiliating deportations. A terrifying panorama, without a doubt. But what about the survivors, those who returned to their countries year after year to brag about their new lifestyles? The day laborers were never too interested in learning English; they would let their bosses speak to them in choppy, rude Spanish or through interpreters. Sometimes they wanted to learn, but they couldn't; at other times, they could, but there was always something better to do than go to classes. That's not even mentioning their closed-mindedness, their delight about what made them suffer, their superstitions, and their absolute lack of sincerity. They would even become traitors to their beliefs, and there was no lack of adherents to the Virgin who would change sides and join some Illuminist sect and start preaching in favor of work and money, and against the sins that he knew from experience. Sooner or later, the law of minimal effort would prevail. Single men would live crowded together in guesthouses or small rooms that were sometimes the property of their bosses. When they weren't working, they bummed around the house, lazing away the day. The most obsessive ones saved up for ostentatious used cars, luxury items, electrical apparatuses, or transactions with a coyote. Young or old, simian copies of what they watched on television, they would dress up with remnants of fashion purchased from swap meets. Full of evangelical optimism while at work, they would feign disinterest in the dive bars they would frequent on their days off. They would return to their countries each winter, and they would return each spring to seasonal jobs, without money and with hangovers that would last until summer. They would complain, but the dollar's an addiction. They would send money back home, but they would never consider a permanent return to the homeland. With time and luck, they would turn into small-time impresarios and idols in their native towns. They maintained an entrepreneurial and greedy spirit, ready to sacrifice anything just to land a spot working. "Why are you still here?" I would ask them when they would mumble and moan. Dollars, comfort, and astonishingly efficient infrastructure. Who could resist bragging about his prosperity?

I worked my ass off just like them and I never complained because they were the first ones to test me. Working alongside them, each task proved to be a lonely and tough affair, until I proved my mettle and that I wasn't going to desert my job. They were bent on destroying anyone who threatened their jobs with scheming and other tricks.

Parrot had given me my fake papers, but with my birthdate making me seven years younger. The signatures on the work permit and Social Security card looked as it they had been scrawled by a second grader. All in all, though, the papers seemed passable.

$

"I forgot to ask you when you were born. I guessed at your age and signed for you," Parrot said.

That same Tuesday night, the chef stopped serving a couple of hours earlier than usual; it was around two in the morning on a rather slow shift. I had finished washing a battery of enormous aluminum pots and had hooked them above the stoves. It was the least they expected of me. Nobody complained, but everyone else seemed to work harder. They were oiled up with pride itself. All the while I worked there I barely had the opportunity to size up the dimensions of the kitchen. We were able to move about with ease, but nobody stepped over the boundaries of his workstation. Each to his own, ignoring what was going on elsewhere. Waiters and busboys came down for their orders, and they shouted some praise at us if only to hurry us on, as their tips were at risk.

I remembered when I worked as a butcher at an expensive restaurant in Mexico City, how the waiters would toss us a few bones gathered from their tips. Here, hell no. We should be grateful that they even spoke to us. There was a red-haired waiter of Greek origin who would rush down the stairs each night, get down on one knee, throw us kisses, extending his arms, as if he were on the Broadway stage, all while shouting: "Thank you!" He would respond to our catcalls by inviting us to go out with him. He was always in a good mood, and he called all of us Pepes. One of the cooks gave him the nickname Puputo. It was the only word in Spanish that he understood.

Upon finishing my job, I went to the changing area. The Puerto Rican was there asking if anyone wanted to wash the shelves in the refrigerator the size of a guestroom on the rooftop, in order to place the meat, vegetables, and rest of the food that they had used during the day. Afterward, the volunteer would have to gather all the work uniforms, separate them, and then bring them up to the truck for linen service. The guy in charge of this hadn't shown up. He started his shift when Parrot did. No one answered. They continued to quickly change, ready to get home. I raised my hand, and without glancing around to see if anyone else would do it, I received the extra pay, and I went to the restaurant to get to work.

I had to go up the stairs. The kitchen was in the basement of a twenty-three-story building. I finished almost three hours later, drugged from exhaustion. Finally, Parrot, just as drained as myself, offered to leave the bags in exchange for five bucks.

I went outside, walking slowly, my eyes looking like hemorrhoids because of the exposure to extreme heat and cold, and I ran into some of the cooks and kitchen help; they were drinking some beer outside a store before taking the subway. I had the impression they were waiting for me. One of the cooks invited me to take a beer that Arnulfo had bought from the store. Arnulfo: the guy as compact as a propane tank who couldn't explain how to prep the salads and desserts. He communicated via gestures made with his stumpy hands. "Ya just toss in that thingamajob, and then that one there, and then this thingy here, okay?" He would also provide me with the names of the ingredients, chopping up words, and he would wrap up his lesson quickly, attempting to be so fast I couldn't follow him. By my third day at work, I was fed up, and I asked the chef to finally explain things so I could be left alone. "That's why you got Arnulfo, ask him," he said to me, annoyed, while he finished. I learned everything else by trial and error, having to put up with the scolding from Poblano.

A twenty-four-ounce can. I started to slurp at it. The rest were making plans to end the night by dancing at a place in Queens. The head cook looked at me.

"How's the fucking job?"

"I'm getting along."

"Good. I can see you haven't been doing this long. In the beginning you want to help and make a good impression. But the problem is you make everyone else look bad. Because everyone else wants their day to end. Once the boss says to turn off the ovens, you got to put things in place and clean quickly so we can scram, just like you saw. If they want to clean the kitchen, let them do it tomorrow. That's their load. As far as we're concerned, once it's three, we're out of there. Let's go! Am I right or am I wrong?"

"You're dead right," I responded with that neutral look tattooed on my face twenty-four hours a day.

"Just imagine if we left everything, the pots and pans, the uniforms, all in a mess. Nobody would help you. Just imagine when you would finish. You can see that the job's a tough one and we got to do things quickly. If we're making more than we need to eat, then we're doing well."

I agreed. In my circumstance, any argument was better than one I could come up with. I lit a cigarette, and it's almost as if I had fainted. I started to see little lights sparkle and a cold sweat gave me goose bumps. The absolute depletion of any energy had me so drugged that I didn't even pay attention to a black man who was tugging at my jacket sleeve, asking for some change. After insulting me, he walked away in a strange zigzag, bowlegged, looking like he was a pedaling a bicycle.

I finished the beer and the cigarette. I chucked the empty can into the store's trash bin. Then we silently walked toward the subway. On my way home, I looked at the bright signs and billboards that I had ignored previously.

Most of them lived in Queens, on Roosevelt Avenue, crammed in with Mexicans and Colombians. Once we were on the platform, everyone found a spot. While I waited for the train, one of the cooks in charge of the main stove approached me.

"So what's up, you're not coming with us to dance?"

"It's real late. I'd rather sleep."

He made a gesture with his index finger and thumb, suggesting that I had smoked some weed. I said I hadn't. He started to laugh and he told the others, who were looking at us from a few feet away. The train arrived and I wait for them to board and leave. I wanted to gather myself together, and in case I needed help, I didn't want to ask help from those who tried their best to stay as far away as possible from the police.

The platform was empty. While gazing into the darkness of the tunnel, my anxiety increased. The F line was filled with thick yellow lines. I soon heard voices and footsteps on some metallic surface, but no one was walking down to the platform. At that time of night, the subway was a catacomb and anyone walking around on the platform looked like a prisoner. I made myself feel better by reasoning that I wouldn't have to struggle finding a seat. I could choose a spot where I could stretch out for the thirty-five-minute ride home. I had already learned to always respect the space of young black riders at that hour; they would mark out their territory with insults and loud, riotous laughter.

I located the signs for the different routes and ways to reach the trains in a type of disturbing dream. My lips were chapped, and my body itched as if with a rash. I was hot, yet exposed to a hellish chill on the platform. I was disconnecting myself from everything except for the route that would bring me to my bed. That's how I finished my shift each night until I deserted work after two months.

PART II
CONNECTICUT

CHAPTER EIGHT

In which...the Artist is reborn as a nanny...
"Property should be used to get you out of sticky
situations"...the Artist meets Fred, an actual parrot...
shocking fridge memos are exposed!

I ended up in Greenwich, Connecticut, following a trail blazed by Norma. Her experiences and pigheadedness in a certain way helped reap some rewards for us both. From so much flipping through newspapers, telephone calls, comparing and contrasting, getting ready for interviews where she would always haggle for fewer hours yet higher pay, Norma had reached a point where she could choose what best suited her, and she could even advise others on options. She knew the market for black-market jobs better than anyone else. She knew the habits and mentality of the patrons like any FBI agent.

Norma's efficiency had earned the attention of people she knew, and she enjoyed showing them, without charging a fee, what they could find just by setting aside their complexes and apprehensions. She recommended me to a family in the Cos Cob area, urged on by a household supervisor who also cooked for the two boys and their father, who was named Gunter. When that individual approved hiring me, I spent most of my time with Patricia, his Irish ex-wife who put on aristocratic airs.

Gunter was the vice president of a bank in New York, and he made frequent trips to Germany, his native country.

They paid me $200 per week with a check made out to his oldest son to avoid any suspicions or hassle when cashing the check, as the tellers always asked for an official ID or proof of legal, permanent residence, which of course I didn't have; moreover, they debated with the supervisor if I should be paid an amount that seemed suspicious for someone who claimed to not be working.

The first time I went to the bank, the manager called Gunter's office to verify that I was part of an international "exchange program" and that my "sponsor" had asked me to cash his check. The manager agreed to do it as a favor, but not before advising Gunter that the bank found it necessary to know every little detail before forking over the cash.

The most important thing for Gunter was to avoid taxes and especially any immigration agents. His son shouldn't stir up any suspicion that they had hired undocumented workers. Patricia lived in the exclusive, woody hills of the town, and she visited us on Fridays at noon. No one exactly knew what she did for a living. Gunter would lean back in ironic laughter when addressing the matter with his boys.

"A beautiful neighborhood. A charming home. Good contacts. Shopping on Fifth Avenue. Jesus Christ! How does she do it? What she got from our divorce isn't enough for all of that!"

For a year, Patricia gave me a weekly bonus in cash, which she stuffed in an envelope that smelled of Chanel perfume. She did this secretly, and I never wanted to know why. Patricia set up strict boundaries when it came to her intimate life, and it was in keeping with her despotic and manipulative character to do so, especially if one of the boys wished to pry more into her daily routine. The most she would ever fess up to, yet in a menacing tone softened by cordial diction she had learned in a prep school for little Irish ladies, was that she worked as the personal assistant to a millionaire. Sure you do.

We would sip coffee and eat French-style pastries during the awkward interrogation. Frequently, she would invite us to eat at restaurants in town or at her home.

Patricia's fortune exceeded both the incomes and possessions combined of the majority of people I had met until then. Her clothes that she wore on a daily basis would cost half my year's income. She was a generous hostess who made no distinctions between myself and her sons. She knew that I loved choice filets—besides, it was the only thing her sons would eat without making faces—and she would serve them bathed in gravy, accompanied by a salad and a dressing she had prepared. The desserts and Colombian coffee soon followed. She would offer me some wine like someone confessing a crime to which she would pay for by way of life imprisonment. *No thanks, Patricia, I prefer your gaze of a bitch in heat, while you tell me vague stories about your self-destructive weaknesses.* She was my Mrs. Robinson who was hungering for two eggs served Mexican style. The sparkle in her eyes reflected a composure always on the brink of spinning out of control. "Smoking in the garden is allowed," she would say, while she opened the windows and then excused herself to prepare coffee.

Patricia loved it when we would agree to take a splash in the pool during hot summer afternoons. She would prepare lemonade adorned with lemon peels and she would set it on the garden table, on a tray holding crystal glasses with delicate green and blue tonalities, cloth napkins, and fruit.

She once asked me to set up a small fence made from nylon along the rill that went through her property. The objective was to make it so migrant ducks wouldn't invade her garden and pool.

While I concentrated on doing my best job, I started to feel a suffocating anxiety that I recognized as rage. My mother had grown up in an orphanage in Guadalajara. Her explosive and enraged character owed a lot to a life filled with privations, which was prolonged by having children. She died from an embolism at an age when other women like Patricia start obsessing about getting face-lifts. Fifteen years later, faithful to his own style of doing so, my father died. He worked all of his life without making any true gains from his talent as a jeweler. He was a role model and a teacher to many apprentices who, just like him, immigrated to the United States, following him to where he worked as the head of a workshop owned by Jews who ended up employing twenty-five top-notch artisans, all of them Mexican and, with the passing of time, all of them proudly *pocho*. During that bonanza period, when my father was overtaken by nostalgia, he'd dress my older brothers like funk musicians. They would sport satin shirts in shrill colors and with ballooned sleeves, the likes of which I would later see on a show that aired music videos each Sunday and in rock magazines. The younger siblings received beautiful toys. The gifts reached us by plane, whenever my father's friends returned to visit their families. Unlike these friends of his, my father soon did away with the extreme productivity in that Texas town, and after three years he came home to Mexico City with savings, anxious about the new life he was going to start.

The bonanza didn't last long. Bad family business ideas, and especially the devaluations, ended the harmony. My parents could name all the pawnshops. They transmitted their experiences to us as if by osmosis. "Property should be used to get you out of sticky situations" was the family motto. My mother's children grew used to living on the installment plan. Filling our stomachs was the priority. Until the last days of his life, my father was a mordant reader of the evening papers and of certain novels and spiritual books: *The Christ of Calvary, The Bible Was Correct*. When I was ten, he made me read *The Old Man and the Sea* and *All Quiet on the Western Front*. We had a book collection revolving around shocking crimes, and they were my favorite, even if they gave me nightmares. One of my sisters worked in a children's bookstore, and she would take me with her every Saturday to leave me in the reading room on the second floor. I would spend the mornings there reading, never moving from my little bench and table. On payday, she would give me illustrated books with typography suited for the myopic: fables, adventure stories, battles at sea. My father was convinced that I was ill, and to top things off, I was left-handed. "We need to tie that boy's left hand so he learns how to eat correctly." "Stop reading, you look like you're a sleepwalker." "Why don't you go out and play with the other kids?" He didn't know what he was doing. Here I am.

That cycle opened and closed in lugubrious neighborhoods. My parents were stubborn about life despite the fact that they were shown the uselessness of any business if it didn't come accompanied by some sort of trick or scam, all of which proved to be part of our sentimental education. They were never ready to accept the reality they faced, and at the same time, when it came to our achievements and celebrations, we would curse each other out, fired up by absurd responsibilities that they would heap upon us even if they dealt with matters that our combined efforts couldn't combat.

My siblings formed their own families according to the familiar way. Only now they drove modest cars and lived in rented apartments or government-subsided housing in dismal neighborhoods, anxious about their jobs or long stretches of unemployment. The genetic lottery had tenaciously provided things so that we would twist back into our own anger. The younger siblings learned trades and took on jobs that let us understand exactly what it was like to be in prison like some of our neighbors and friends. The faith in university degrees that my siblings inculcated in their children would only, and with great difficulty, provide them with something more than their inheritance of belonging to a family of paid-by-the-hour scoundrels.

I barely realized that I was panting, choking on the past. Because of the stifling heat, I was glazed with sweat as if I had been working outside all day. I refused to recognize what was filling me up with so much rage. My Banana Republic T-shirt was drenched with sweat smelling of Givenchy cologne. I had been turned into a servant with a luxury uniform, thanks to the presents from a wealthy family.

I finished setting up the fence, and under the guise of returning a hammer I didn't use to the garage, I stayed inside there, calming myself. I felt trapped in my rage and wanted to shatter the windows of the convertible Audi. I saw in the reflection some guy with reddened eyes. *Accept what you are: a bitter person. You just remembered where you came from, now give them the pretext. Come, walk back to sixteen years ago. "If you don't take care of your kids, next time, it's juvenile hall." You remember? That was the warning that a social worker gave to your father who had gone to grease his palm so that you and your brother wouldn't be sent to a boot camp for youth along with all the other young hoods.*

To eat filets and earn some dollars, I had to work for some people who had no merit other than being kind in exchange for not loading them down with guilt and a solitude that turned them touchy and implacable when it came to my pride. With an astute sense of finances, they filled their houses up as if they were halls exhibiting everything that could compose a monumental tackiness. Perhaps that's why they kept me on a loose leash. I was their best house alarm. They didn't seem to learn from their personal tragedies. They referred to their egoism as "each one for himself." Fucking bullshit! I knew about that pride, only from the opposite angle. I kept myself alert by the morbid interest of Patricia in me; unsatisfied with my curt or mordant answers, she would do additional investigations with the children when I wasn't around. It wasn't necessary to lie or avoid questions to keep her away from my past, anguishes, or interests. What a world like hers stirred any interest in me. She would never understand my hatred for the job, nor why I never said thanks for anything. I returned to the pool and I sat down to get some sun and sip some lemonade, making a toast to Patricia.

Her boys laughed at her pretentions, prattle, and lack of culture. I once urged Pete to ask his mother if she knew that Jonathan Swift was a travel agent in Ireland. She answered yes.

Patricia politely reminded me to not bring guests home. She was the one who had suggested to Gunter to change the gender of the nannies and housekeepers. The nannies prior to my arrival allowed themselves to be groped for money, and they robbed all sorts of junk, especially a Frenchwoman who would screw her boyfriend in the kitchen and would always leave dirty maxi pads in the bathroom.

"You're not a fag, right?" asked Gunter when I was interviewed.

"Why, you into Mexican guys?" I answered at once, swallowing my anger. His boys laughed wildly and the old man was forced to admit he had been one-upped.

It was the best job I had for years. I lived at ease thanks to the boys; they were happy to have found an eager accomplice to their frequent saturnalias of music, drugs, beer, video games, and board games with friends who, at night, would climb up to Michael's window to avoid Kaiser, the German shepherd being trained as a guard dog, and Gunter. These gatherings were like a déjà vu of a stage in my life that I had left behind long ago.

During the start of the 1980s, the majority of us skipped school regularly, and we would go to ditching parties at houses or warehouses, where we would cough up some cash for buckets of beer. The main idea was to dance until dawn to music that was in style. Some dude with a microphone would act as the MC, greeting his acquaintances or announcing a new beat. The MC also acted as an intermediary between rowdy groups. Among the people I knew were some brothers whom I played tennis with on courts that we painted in the parking lots of the housing complexes where we lived. They were sullen and conscientious, especially when it came to keeping score. They never beat me. Their parents had a lunch counter in one of the malls, and they also sold knickknacks smuggled in from the United States. One day, Don Neto came up with the idea of getting some turntables, a small mixer, and some "limited" records that he hoped his sons could resell for a higher price. That's when the story of the Winners sound started. First at his house, the dad would charge entry fees and sell small bottles of Coke and cigarettes. It was just a bunch of us bums without much money to spend a night somewhere else. We would laugh at the brothers, who looked as if they had been lobotomized while they groped at their consoles and records. Sometimes I would approach them and ask for a rock song; they would respond to my request by sticking up their middle fingers.

After three months, the house proved to be too small. Their father paid off a patrol car to watch the street. They ended up renting the game room. Shortly after, without any better options that would ensure not being caught by raids, we all reluctantly attended the parties at warehouses and wedding halls. We spent entire nights trying to make girls who weren't interested, something that I considered fun for a bunch of pansies and dandies with money to burn. I never got any, and I covered up my loudmouthed loneliness with drugs and wild binges that had me returning home on the verge of total collapse. I idolized rock, the louder the better. The Ramones and the Clash were my patron saints who kept me away from the pretentious girls and frequent cold showers. However, within those vast halls lit up with strobe lights and revolving disco balls, there was a bounding energy that, despite my disposition, made me feel joyous. With no one to follow along on a stage as he made rude gestures, spoke drivel, or did acrobatic moves with his guitar, one could let oneself be taken over by the music, moving one's body in a way that would have been considered feminine back then, but which attracted women. It all had a lot to do with a demented and cruel hedonism, yet instead of provoking aggression, it left the listeners in a type of trance. If I had been more sincere with myself, I would have leaped onto the dance floor and gotten closer to one of the many girls dancing alone, yet stayed in the middle of a circle of types like myself: confused, sadist, completely wasted, or simply possessing a guillotining hatred. The sounds of the Winners and their contemporaries, the Polymarchs, turned them into the preachers of disco in the slums and small towns. With the passing of time, their legend grew, just like the tonnage of their equipment, which they used to echo throughout stadiums and sports arenas for around forty thousand people.

Marcel and Jeff were two other brothers, but with Colombian parents. They would bring their records and equipment to Michael's room. They had the same intense passion for music and for lighting enormous pipes filled with marijuana that would have us on the brink of madness while we watched them mix on the turntables. Supposing that I was some sort of alley cat imported from an enormous city surrounded by pyramids, plots of cannabis, and horny, curvaceous women, Marcel, the more extroverted and knowledgeable of the two, would patiently explain the finer details of a music that, to my ears, sounded as if it had been lifted from my adolescence. During four raw winters, the DJs and their emotional autism made sense to me. Snow would fall outside Michael's bedroom window while we smoked some thick joints rolled by Jeff. The patio was covered by mud. In the black shadows, light glistened from neighboring houses. The snowstorms raised white hills more than three feet high, and the weather forecast reported at least three more weeks of blizzards, mud, and ice slicks. Classes were canceled. Winter clothes piled up by the bedroom doors. The porch thermometer indicated that it was fifteen below, and stepping outside to the street proved to be a lost battle after just a few steps.

Around that time, a block of ice destroyed the back window of Gunter's car when it was parked beneath the train's bridge. Jeff and Marcel had walked two and a half miles from their house. The streets and freeways were closed off or with access reserved only for emergency vehicles. The trucks that would dredge the streets of ice didn't help. However, Jeff and Marcel arrived, carrying backpacks stuffed with equipment, early on Friday night, ready to play the best from their song list, which they continually tinkered with at a specialty discotheque fifteen miles north of Greenwich. I was stretched out on the comfortable leather sofa, and I tried to capture the change in beats and their sense. Marcel liked experimenting, and he sometimes mixed old *cumbia* and *vallenata* records, which he took from his father's collection, a baker at the factory in Port Chester. Jeff's strength lay in house and, according to what others said, he had a future in the scene: he was one of the local stars, regionally celebrated in the raves of Connecticut and Upstate New York. Marcel, younger and more intuitive, professed a sick love for his brother, and he took care to not overshadow him while he worked at the turntables. Marcel pretended to learn things from Jeff when he had already learned them by ear. They took turns with their pipes and made the records spin, and they invited me to follow along, my brain with hundreds of burned-out fuses, but with enough still crackling to accept the fact that that was the perfect music for cold cities, polar ones, where one had to stay inside to protect oneself from winter's sadism. Traveling through an interior world with vibrant colors and friendly energy made us feel like we were inhabitants of Interzone, just like the old pirates imagined it, even Bill B: out of the reach of civilization, but with a *deus-jockey* making his modest omnipresence known through break beats. The world could get lodged in the ice age. We had all we needed to sample to our liking.

$

During the day, I took advantage of the fact no one was around to take long naps, read, and use the computer. During the night, some classes awaited me, as well as time at a bar. I ate well from the enormous two-door refrigerator from which— as according to Gunter's instructions—I had to toss still-fresh food into the trash, yet which no one had touched. It never took me more than four hours to do my duties, which were always the same, and I even ended up developing a soft spot for their household pets, especially Fred, an enormous parrot with a potbelly and near-human intelligence. Every morning, Fred patiently employed his beak to open the hinge to his cage, and then he would help Brad, the canary, do the same. Then, while his companion flapped about scared, Fred walked down the plank splattered with greenish shit, dodging my projectiles to reach the bowl of Kaiser's food, which he would pick at as if it were sunflower seeds. I would wait awhile from an armchair while I ate corn on the cob, and I would then chuck them at his potbelly. In order to catch him, I would use an iron poker that I slid under his claws.

Torpid and obese, Fred would vent his frustration via shrill squawks, moving his head about as if he were recuperating from a knockout while returning defeated to his corner of the cage. Although Brad was more stupid and cowardly, he was also more agile, and it would take me a longer time to catch him, as he was still light enough to fly. Both resigned themselves to waiting for the day's end while shrieking *uuuaaakk uuuaaakk*. Gunter took charge of liberating them again and spoiling them with cookies and slices of apples.

Until a little before my arrival at the home, there were telephone lines in each bedroom to assign and argue about duties, a result of Gunter's stinginess and his children. Gunter slept in a bedroom on the first floor; his closet was filled to the brim with clothes, his desk was covered with bills he had to pay, expensive knickknacks, and a panoramic television that he kept on all night.

I would jump onto his king-size bed late each morning to make phone calls while I watched TV. When he returned from work, Gunter would slip on some underwear and a white T-shirt. At dawn, you could hear Gunter's sheepskin Apache-style moccasins walking the plank from his bedroom to the kitchen for food. Suit, shoes, and shirt would remain at the foot of his bed until the following day, when I would bring them to the washing machine and the dry cleaner's. Next to his bedroom was the "studio" with two cages that I could fit into if I knelt down. They were the lodgings of Fred and Brad.

From my small room way up in the attic, I clearly heard and triangulated the telephone conversations. I was the first to ward off Gunter in the remote case that it occurred to him to go up and see what his boys did during the night. If I couldn't stop him, Pete would come, and he would amuse him in his bedroom facing the hallway by cracking some joke he had heard at school or showing some new riffs he had learned on his out-of-tune guitar, while Michael hid the bongs, sprayed air freshener in the room, and did his best to make the room look like a hurricane hadn't hit it. If his friends didn't have enough time to hide in the closet, which had a door to the garage, they would sit quietly on the soft leather sofa, staring at the television screen with eyes as red as a rabbit's from marijuana.

"Michael," Gunter said, while making his voice resonate as if he were addressing an audience. "What is this? A billiard hall? Open the windows and make sure your friends don't stay too late." Then he turned to me. "I didn't know you liked that goddamn noise," he said, referring to the music. I was protecting myself within the darkness of the hallway, keeping a certain distance from Gunter so he wouldn't notice my eyes or how I reeked of whiskey. Morning, I heard him walk down the plank; his moccasins entered and exited the kitchen with plates for him and Kaiser, who slept by his side, on the floor. I embarked on an epistolary enmity with Gunter that proved to be convenient as it avoided arguments. Many memos were taped to the refrigerator, such as the following:

> *As I asked you a while ago, you must thoroughly clean the house each day, including the bath-rooms and the boys' bedrooms. Sweep and clean the birds' room and don't lock them up in their cages, as they're very nervous and do themselves harm. Prepare the recipe that I left you here. Tell Pete to buy me some Cokes and for him to not forget to feed Kaiser and the birds.*
>
> *—Gunter*

> *Gunter: I clean the house* <u>till it's spotless</u> *every day. You don't notice this because your foul dog and parrot make sure to mess up what I took all morning to clean. The same with your kids. If you want to see your house clean when you get home, starting tomorrow I will keep Kaiser in*

*the backyard and the birds inside their cages. I
don't see Pete during the day. You'd be better off
calling his friends.*

*P.S. The meat you bought at Grand Union was
very tough and I gave it to the dog. Careful with
that mad cow disease.*

And such was how each day transpired. My personality
matched his beliefs about "Mexicans." I trusted him, but not
much.

CHAPTER NINE

Regional Trains of the Tri-State Area

I spent two years attending night classes on an irregular basis in the north of Connecticut, in Norwalk. Twenty minutes driving an old Toyota up Highway 95. After my English classes, I got a kick out of visiting bars and diners. I put the pedal to the metal, making the engine strain as I chose one of the detours through any town on the way home. With no idea how to try something different, I had decided to work at any hour in whatever came my way.

I frequently would take a train to Grand Central in Manhattan. During the week, Amtrak mainly transported office workers and businessmen. Those travelers represented suburban progress. With mortgaged property and enough credit to go around, many traveled chained to their laptops and workweek boredom. With the same efficient tone of voice, they conversed about their families or sports in the same manner that they agreed to appointments and business transactions on their cell phones. They never regarded the rest of the passengers without some sort of bovine gaze. But that was one achievement of the democracy in which they were raised: masters and their servants traveled in the same wagon.

During peak hours, one could board trains with all-night bar service. After a trip somewhere between thirty-five minutes and an hour and fifteen minutes, depending on one's station, those men and women who made ruthless financial decisions would get off the trains, faces swollen with fatigue, checking their briefcases several times to make sure they didn't leave anything behind on the train. After a long day, the drinks gave them the courage necessary to face the simpleminded home life, replete with shouting arrogant children with braces, piles of mail—utility bills, mortgage payments—the wife glued to the telephone, and maids sent from countries pawned by the World Bank.

I came from a country that had no need to be saved in a military way, as it shared its border with the boss. Sometimes I felt like a special offer from *National Geographic* delivered to one's door.

During holidays, Amtrak transported hundreds of cooks, waiters, maids, grannies, bricklayers, sickly people, cripples, drug addicts, alcoholics, and unemployed folk, who could only be so on a full-time basis or by receiving remuneration for temp jobs. During the summer, the presence of rich kids was a familiar thing. They assaulted New York City to consume alcohol and drugs before returning home on the last trains running from Grand Central. At their destination stops there were vans waiting for them. All of this reminded one of the metro in Mexico City, yet without yuppies. Maids, bricklayers, buck privates on leave, hunchbacks, and workers; entire families coming and going from the Chapultepec, the Alameda, or some prison; and members of the middle class on their way down to poverty. Both spectrums of local customs also included the rapist, the alcoholic, the drug addict, the prostitute, the nymphomaniac, the "unfeeling jackal," the tax evader, and the stateless traveler. However, what was different from the Mexican metro—where the racial mix provoked discrimination against different registers of language and clothing worn—was that in the Amtrak the people working as conductors were black or white with names ending with "-osky." They were resigned to their category as losers with legal working status. Their salaries were almost as pathetic as undocumented workers who would travel on the trains, yet they could brag that they were children of Uncle Sam, and with benefits. Perhaps that explains their pretentiousness; instead of just checking or taking tickets, they also served as immigrant police who kept guard on deported travelers.

The electric light inside the train made us look paler, while we spread out in the plush seats. Upon boarding a train, we would run to a seat where we could stretch out our legs, lie down, or make a traveling picnic with hamburgers, hot dogs, cupcakes, coffee, beer, soda, even tacos. Before the train set off, bums would get on board to collect empty cans and newspapers, which they would later trade in for cash. They would do so quickly, and they would curse if you didn't raise your feet so they could check beneath your seat.

The train cars were more or less clean, despite the stink from the bathrooms and the scraps of food that had been piling up all day. The train conductors would make a fuss if you didn't take off your shoes before resting your feet on the seat in front of you, but they rarely complained about any of the preexisting putrid odors on the train. They would collect tickets with a type of mute resentment for a job that provoked no emotions, now that the trains rarely suffered any breakdowns, derailments, or delays, even during snow season.

Our faces reflected where we came from, where we were headed, and what we thought about our lives. Everyone was silent, never addressing anyone else unless if one was lost and needed directions. Some rested, others gazed into the emptiness, and those with less time in the country were overwhelmed by worrying, trying to figure out the announcements echoing from loudspeakers for the next station or train connection.

One Sunday during the start of September, I returned from Manhattan on the last train out. I had spent the weekend in the Bronx. Tired, my ears ringing, and my sense of reasoning worked up into a dark frenzy—the results of a gnarly hangover—I boarded the train behind a group of university students, tall, blond, and dressed up as if they were counselors at a camp. Normal looking and drunkards. Two of them, with beers in hand, shared seats with a black passenger who looked like Louis Armstrong when he accentuated his poverty with bugged eyes. They listened to music on Walkmans at a deafening volume. Two stations later, at Pelham, a group of girls modeled after characters on *Beverly Hills, 90210* boarded the train. They flaunted their firm and tan thighs beneath their denim shorts. One of them wanted to be a flirt, and ignoring the conversation of her equally attractive friends, she starting poking fun at the one listening to a Walkman. He understood that she was talking about him, and they stole glances at each other, before they snuggled up into the same spot. The girl looked at me and made a polite request. I gazed at her with the look of an idiot to minimize my shock. She set off to the rear door, lifted herself up on a handlebar, locked her heels together, and began to swing back and forth as if she were going to fling herself into the void.

Outside, in the unanimous darkness, opal flashes ran in the opposite direction of the train. The beery drowsiness of the friends and the available girls became more apparent as they started to chatter loudly. The blonde recognized one of the guys who mumbled in his sleep. She immediately approached him, plopped herself astride his thighs, raised his cap with a university's emblem, shook his shoulders, shouted his name into his ear several times, pulled on his tie, rubbed herself against him repeatedly. Nothing. The rest encouraged this with the cheering and laughter of someone peeking through a keyhole at cheerleaders. They huddled together nervously.

The chosen one preferred to keep on drooling, despite the fact that that flirtatious groping was superior to any act done by one's self, which is where the adventure ended. At the Harrison station, before getting off the train, the girl shouted her name and phone number, and told the friends of the stoic traveler for him to call her as soon as he woke up and that she would be waiting for his call. The girls took the only fantasy on board with them as they exited. A black man returned to his previous posture and raised the volume on his Walkman. The boy wearing the cap pried one eye open and laughed at the jokes his friends were making about his not "waking up." The incident with the blonde proved to me that I was no different from any of the other passengers on board.

Port Chester, a promiscuous and divided city. That's where the state of New York ended. The southern edge of the city was where black and Latino residents shared their lives of poverty. The northern part was for the white residents. The train crossed the state line into Connecticut on one of the many bridges that permitted a passenger to guess at the simple layout of the city—that is, where the rock clubs were located, and the Caribbean dance halls, the wine shops, and the bars, the Catholic Cross and the Anglican church, the police station and the Salvation Army. As if those multicolored signs floated beneath the train.

I reached Cos Cob, a lonely station in Greenwich. Its gloomy, tree-lined roads hid a millionaire suburb without any delinquency on its streets. Calm and functional. I perceived the soothing sensation of walking in a night where the emptiness on the street replaced fear.

$

At the end of the summer, Patricia invited me to go to Ireland to meet her family. The only condition was that I stick to her kids while she engaged in her social life. I said yes, although I forgot to mention that I might have problems when trying to reenter the country, as the legal duration of my visit had expired long ago; however, my passport and visa were still valid, so I had a good chance of getting a new stamp for six months from customs in Ireland. Norma and other workers had done the same thing with success at JFK Airport. All in all, there was nothing positive about possibly being deported to Mexico.

When we reached Ireland, Patricia handed me another perfumed envelope with $100 "just in case you and the boys need anything." In overcast Ireland, I spent those dollars, and many more, in all the pubs in plain sight.

In one of them, on O'Connell Street, the main drag, Simonne made a lunch date for the boys and me before taking our first tour of the city. She was Patricia's niece. They didn't get along. They both tried to maintain their composure, but Simonne faltered where the other one stood her ground. Simonne was the youngest of Sean's two daughters; he was an ex-priest who had fallen in love with a redhead after months of hearing her give confession. The redhead worked as a secretary at the diocesan magazine where he was the editor. Both resigned from their previous lives in order to get married, but one day, when Simonne was eight, her mother disappeared without leaving a trace. Sean spent some years inside of pubs and AA meetings before becoming a scriptwriter for radio dramas that aired on BBC. While this was going on, he started to take notice of Patricia's sister, Ann, a meddlesome, timorous, pious soul who did acts of charity in the churches and hospitals of the slums. That's how she expiated for the sin of living in concubinage. Ann never missed an opportunity to recommend the book of memories by "His Holiness," especially when she detected a hangover. Sean had to sleep each night with Golgotha right next to him.

Simonne was terrified of old age; according to her, the only way to avoid it was by drinking until you burst. She could turn a good joke into a melodrama over several pints of Kilkenny. "Only old men drink Guinness": that was one of her ambiguous and fleeting phrases she repeated. She was referring to her father. She always found a way of getting money, and her friends, most of them police officers and tireless braggarts, would always joke like a group of teenagers about which one was going to sleep with her whenever she got up to go to the restroom. In her jeans and old cardigan sweater, she apparently had no interest in sex.

Simmone depended on her sister for everything. She would call her on the phone no matter the hour or where we were. "Oh, Nicole! Thank God I found you! Are you okay?" And then she would relate all of her recent activities, as if she hadn't seen her for years. Then she would whisper gossip, on the verge of tears, and with a look on her face as if she were deranged. She was always scared about things, but she ended up angry. She knew everybody's story, and thanks to her I learned about a dark and offsetting Dublin. We drank all day and night. All the pubs downtown were identical. In all of them, the people smelled the same, and they all wore that look of having been heartbroken. The other pubs, on the waterfront, offered the same thing, but with rock music blasting in the background. After a few days, Michael and Pete got bored, and they finished their vacation inside their uncle's home. When Patricia and the boys returned to the States, I decided to stay on with the family in my attic room. No one seemed to mind.

Once, I was inside a pub, the tables and bar crowded, surrounded by rugby players; the men and women having fun by watching the idols of Irish families on a variety show playing on an enormous screen. Before the pub burst out into song, I would have thought that I was witnessing a parody of some sappy, gay rock group. At dawn, after vomiting in my room, I fell asleep with one of the catchy tunes of a group that called themselves Mama's Boy ringing in my ears.

Simmone and Nicole dreamed of reuniting with their mother. She had abandoned them to go to South Africa with another woman. She told them everything in a long letter that she sent to one of the parishes where Ann lent her services. Upon telling me, Simmone made the gesture of a sad and pleading clown in debt to a guilt-inducing and secretive religiosity. At other times, she gazed into her habitual lies regarding her disappearances that lasted for days. She found jobs reserved for day laborers, except it was odd, as local day laborers were nearly nonexistent. Ireland exported them to other countries. It was the same as in other places; there were thousands of people who needed someone to take care of them, and the best way was to become servants. There's hunger everywhere. The first step is feeling ashamed about setting off at a quick velocity, chasing the carrot.

Once, I met up with Simmone at a pizzeria; I found her inside of the refrigerator peeling garlic, bent over and smoking a cigarette that was dangling from the corner of her lips, which were pale as a corpse's. It was just as easy to get a job as to lose it. Her coquettish, schoolgirl smile would seduce the managers, who would then turn into madmen as a result of her numerous absences, lateness, and excuses after only a few weeks of having been hired. She was the one who came up with the idea of having me stay in Ireland until after the New Year. She would put me in contact with one of her acquaintances and land me a job. "You can stay for as long as you want. *So long, Gunter! Ajua!* We'll travel across Europe. *Cheers!* We'll save our money and visit my mother in South Africa! *Hell yeah!* We'll fuck nonstop! *Come, baby, come! . . ."*

All of that happened at midnight, a little before they threw us out of a pub in downtown Dublin, completely smashed, and without a cent to take a taxi to my hostel. I had her believing that I would prolong my stay while we prolonged our drinking, lies, and fantasies. It was the only moment of euphoria without long stretches of silence, despite the fact that we were crossing the city beneath the rain, in search of a telephone booth where she could down a can of beer while breaking the news to her sister. It was a way of easing things between us.

My bluff liberated us from the sexual tension that had started between us when we first toasted four months before that night. I had the feeling that my life was about to shatter as if it were a glass falling from the hands of a drunkard. I controlled my desire to keep on drinking, and I kept my mouth shut about the pounds that I had saved for my departure the following day. All that time, I had worked a total of twelve hours washing dishes. The restaurant owner decided when and at what time I would work. He was half Italian and half Arabic. The perfect mix to create a pedantic exploiter. A French cook with putrid breath worked next to me in the tiny kitchen. When he approached to instruct me on this or that, I would turn the other way as if I were ignoring him. Don't trust the hungry; they'll betray you when it's time to take vengeance and fill one's belly. I earned a total of thirty-two pounds.

"Don't let them exploit you" was what Simonne's father advised with his typical mocking tone, when I told him about the job on the few occasions that he invited me over for dinner.

That was the only night that Simonne didn't return home to her sister. She came up with me to my attic room. She finished some whiskey while I arranged my remaining luggage; I had sold some while surrounded by garments and knickknacks at a flea market a few days before. Her white lies squeezed drinks and rides from me until the very end, and we went from one end of Dublin to the other, searching for her sister and her friends. We spent a night at one of her friends' houses, taking advantage of the fact that her parents were gone, and each one of us ended up in a different room, as the beer and liquor and marijuana had us crashing at the most convenient spot. I ended up sleeping in a boy's bedroom.

I woke up from an uneasy sleep in the middle of the night hearing the terrorized screaming of a woman. I leaped out of bed thinking something had happened to Simonne. I couldn't remember where I was. I fumbled for the light switch, and when I clicked on the light I realized what it was. I looked out the window: nothing but albatrosses flapping around. I got dressed before going to the living room for a cigarette. Dirty glasses and empty cans were scattered around the rooms. I asked myself who would take the initiative to clean up. I found a half-finished cigarette in a full ashtray. I lit it on the stove, and I sat at the table in the kitchen while looking out the window on the door facing the back patio. I knew darkness hid the sea that separated me from some port in England. I took a final drag, and then I went to the living room for my jacket, scarf, and gloves. Dressed up like a snowman, I left through the kitchen door. I found my way by walking down the avenue parallel to the cove.

Two hours later, beneath one of those blustery and ashen dawns, I returned to downtown Dublin in a bus filled with bums and folks on their way to work. A hangover resulting from the prolonged bacchanalia was about to hit me at any moment. I heard hammer blows inside my head knocking down my walls of resistance. The pubs had proven to be necessary refuges. When the body trembled, asking for alcohol, and the mind asked to flee from danger, there's no room for logic.

Simonne and I didn't even fuck on our last night together. Sex between drunks has no passion and is never sincere. I could see the night behind my shoulders in the mirror on the chest of drawers. My defeated look would facilitate things to get a job. I would have to make the ten pounds in my pocket last while I made my way to the Bronx. Before rushing from the hostel to the Dublin airport, I understood why Simonne preferred to sleep it off rather than saying good-bye.

CHAPTER TEN

**In which...the Artist returns to the Bronx...the Artist
remembers his brother...a new plan emerges.**

> *Even when you self-destruct, you want to fail
> more, lose more, die more than others, stink
> more than others.*
>
> —Don DeLillo, *Cosmopolis*

Norma had left the Bronx for the most famous suburb in the
region of New England. She was hired as a nanny to a family
that, apart from paying her $400 a week, also offered her a
large, furnished studio that was also separate from the house.
No more conflicts with Rose's tenants. No more treacherous
moments to reach a room and fall asleep, still shaking from the
danger on the streets. No more corner drunkards assailing
her for spare change. She found a prefabricated Eden only
forty miles away.

The parsimonious opulence of Greenwich supported
pedantic police officers who directed traffic on the main
thoroughfare as if they were cheerleaders from the academy.
If a pedestrian disobeyed them at the crosswalk, they would
force him to turn around and return to the corner and scold
him.

Upon my return from Ireland, I went to visit Gunter's
children, and they said that Patricia was angry with me. She
accused me of being ungracious. Ann quickly informed her
during my stay in Dublin that I was a bum freeloader and that
I had laughed at her and Sean during Christmas dinner at

their home. It was true, but not in the way she described it. Her husband had invited me a couple of times to the corner pub to rant about the teetotaling and chaste life he led with the aspiring nun. The old guy was a great conversationalist and wise teller of jokes, and he insisted on smooth-talking the young waitresses. We lightened up the silence at the table by joking about the favorite cardinal sins of those women with pious souls who attended church in Dublin. Moreover, Patricia had presumed that I would be at the disposal of her sister. In her reproaches appeared her tyrannical madness when she wanted to put someone in his place. I didn't owe her a thing, and I sent her to hell. Patricia couldn't get an apology from me, and after discussing the matter with Gunter, they came to an agreement to not hire me again. Their children were more upset than I was.

I had to count on Norma for help, despite the fact that she was unbearable whenever I stumbled in life. Over the phone, she told me in detail about the numerous help wanted ads. She never tired of instructing me on the right way to apply for them and how to get around my status as undocumented. I was scared of starting over, and I couldn't stand the idea of living in a town where just by not having a car was enough to make you a criminal suspect. From *A* to *Z*, I found countless reasons why I should remain in the Bronx, but upon reaching the letter *D*, there would appear a triumvirate that would topple any of my arguments: debt, dollars, deficit.

Rose offered me a loan and free housing while I looked for a job. She felt in control of her house again, now that Mark had left for Florida. He had gone looking for one of those roaming caravans that are set up in the middle of nowhere to plant marijuana. Carol disappeared with one of his friends who dressed up like Peter Lorre in *The Maltese Falcon* during their Oscar parties. I promised Rose that I would pay her back sooner than later. Taking her money for lost, Rose advised me to save up what I could and return to Mexico: "Maybe things will work out there." *Of course, since you're not the one in my situation,* I thought while I gave her a loud smooch on her cheek.

I preferred to stay with how things were. I occupied the furnished studio once belonging to her son. I dedicated myself to trail after the ghost of a recent arrival who had no interest in finding work. I had lost thirteen pounds, and the heavy drinking and hashish had poisoned my temperament into one of constant fear. I spent a portion of my money on magazines, books, and food, and I isolated myself like a sick animal scared of being thrashed. The most I did was sleep during the day and cure myself at night by going to the corner bar with Papi's acquaintances.

$

I was watching a movie starring Bette Davis when she knocked on the door. It was a Sunday at dusk. In all honesty, like many people surrounding me, I didn't know how to explain what had made me move thousands of miles from the place where I was born. Days had passed during which I wouldn't leave my room except for cigarettes. I hadn't tasted a drop of alcohol for nearly a month. Dry as a stale dinner roll. But when I went out for a stroll I felt the typical anguish and dizziness associated with a hangover.

I had tried to take advantage of time by correcting drafts and writing new things after three years of having given up. I was bent on trying my luck by sending chronicles to Mexican magazines and newspapers. Writing helped me find time for myself. I was trying to organize my reflections on some of the time I had spent living in the States. My daily fantasies consisted of a lot of money and little work. With my savings, I would open up a bar in Mexico City, one that was like a circus filled with people I had recruited from the streets. My younger brother, Ricardo, would manage the joint, and I would dedicate my time to writing during the day and drinking during the night in that bar of my delirium.

To put it plainly, during the first year of my arrival in the States, I had spent time boxed up like some demented dude who sees and hears but understands nothing. I wanted to return to Mexico and I had plenty of reproaches and excuses to do so, but whenever I earned a hundred bucks after twelve hours of working, I pissed it all away feeling patriotic. I had never earned so much elsewhere for a day's work. During the autumn of my second year living there, I enrolled in an evening class to learn English in a public school for adults filled with day laborers and students who couldn't pass their courses. The successful ones would earn a certificate as specialists in some blue-collar skill that would land them a position with the city or as a low-earning worker in an industrial field. I ended up attending only a few classes in literature. We read stories and novellas, and we wrote short reviews. The class curriculum had no other goal than to make us literate.

My behavior hadn't changed since I was living in Mexico: I couldn't seem to save money; I spent almost all of it, and I held on to receipts and ticket stubs to look for better jobs. That's how I had always been. I lived hand to mouth. Maybe that's why I was always scared.

I opened the door and saw Rose's angular face. She was making gestures and chattering, trying to make me feel happy as if during an intermission. I had let her know ever since we first met that I preferred to be left alone, but she loved to insist. She felt responsible, especially ever since the other renters had left, that I never spent time with her, Joe, and Sandra. While she tried to convince me, I stared absentmindedly at the studio's ragged carpet. For some reason,

I became sensitive to the piercing odor of tobacco lit with my twenty-dollar Zippo.

I suddenly remembered Ricardo; his presence spread open the cool and low-class air that entered through the open windows, just like when he would visit me at my old apartment in the center of Mexico City. He was always smiling although he risked more each day than I did. I remembered those tiny scars of his on his forehead, knuckles, and arms and the other immense ones—almost magnificent—that were furrowed into his belly and torso, hidden beneath the canvas shirt. Neither the chattering of Rose nor *What Ever Happened to Baby Jane?* mattered at that moment, so I turned off the VHS player. It was inevitable that I would serve myself a double. I opened the closet and took out the bottle hidden in a corner and returned to the sofa. This was preferable to Rose's harassment and the din of traffic outside, I said to myself apologetically while I set my cigarette in the ashtray. Just like that time that Ricardo visited me, informing me of the following:

"I won't take up too much of your time; I wanna get home early. I just dropped by to tell you what happened to me yesterday, okay?"

Supposedly I was in a rush to get to a job I found in the newspaper: CLEAN-CUT YOUNG MAN WITH AMPLE KNOWLEDGE OF CULTURE AND YEARNING TO GET AHEAD. MINIMUM OF THREE YEARS IN THE FIELD. LIVING IN THE SOUTHERN PART OF THE CITY. AVAILABLE IMMEDIATELY. NO SALES. REFERENCES NEEDED.

"You know that looking for a job is a waste of time. At least for me. I never have the minimum requirements. But I end up going here and there, filling applications. But when I'm home I watch movies just like you, or I practice on my drum set: *pa, pa, pa, pum, pa, pa, pa, pum...!* That way I can sweat out my hangover. You know that I'm only interested in music. But I don't know what's been going on with me recently. I wake up at dawn when there's nothing on the TV but infomercials for shit that's supposed to make you lose weight, or the news rattling on and on about recent crimes..."

I offered him a cigarette, but he ignored me. I forgot that he was trying to quit. Instead I set out the bottle after taking a swig. We used to do that almost every day. Lots of times we would end up at some police station. More often than not we would find ourselves on some corner, downing a beer. Ricardo's younger than I, and wherever he goes, he gets attention:

"...to be honest, I really do need a job; my room's not cheap, especially for what it looks like...they should pay *me* for living there. Food's not a problem; no one dies of hunger in this city. Like I was saying, I approached the receptionist, but she said the position had been filled, but I could still fill out the application. Just for that the old bitch started making faces. There were some other secretaries there and some fuckers with nervous looks on their faces. Without taking her eyes off the typewriter, that woman told me to call the following week. I left the office, and that chubby woman and one of her security guards watched me to make sure I was getting into the elevator. I felt like a weight had been lifted off my shoulders. I did my duty, right? Things like that never happen to you when you try to get a job. Everyone looked like they were spaced out, as if they were taking a trip inside their own heads and didn't like the landscape. I started walking quickly, just trying to find something to do, and I was laughing that those people were so weird. I reached a café owned by some Chinese people, and I sat at a table with a view of the street. I ordered a soda, but I didn't have money for anything else. I lit a cigarette while hearing two old men talking at the bar. You know, nothing but complaints and schemes to make some quick money. Do this, do that, blah blah blah. I watched the street looking for anything else to distract me, put out my cigarette, then left without paying..."

I laughed while Ricardo put a hand in his pocket and shook the change that was still there. He's corpulent. That's what helped him survive surgery when a .22-caliber bullet pierced one of his lungs. The sudden vibrations coming from stereo speakers in the building next door almost made him lose the thread of his story, but someone lowered the volume, and the trumpets and Caribbean percussion became background music to Ricardo's voice, which had turned hoarse years ago from long hours spent with beer:

"...then I realized I was on my way home. You listenin' to me? Smoke a cigarette on my behalf...There was a bunch of hot chicks walking along, staring at the sidewalk, alone, maybe nervous about all the people and the noise from loudspeakers and traffic. You find a shitload of people on the streets who look like they're both criminals and victims, or at least I can't tell them apart. I guess that's how we look, right? Don't accuse me of being paranoid, but whoever says that we don't needs to be locked up in the nuthouse . . ."

I put out my cigarette butt and took another swig. I agreed with him.

"...it was early, it was barely twilight. I kept walking, and then I reached an avenue with an endless high fence to my right. I thought a country club was behind it. I walked while trying to memorize the names of the streets on the other side: engineers, doctors, architects, attorneys, fucking badasses. There were few people around me; everyone was very pensive as if they wanted to keep it a secret as to how they could live on little money . . ."

That's when I realized that Rose hadn't figured out that I wasn't listening to her. I just kept on saying yes to everything, but my mind was focusing on the years and emotions: the night before the shooting, we got into a fight with one of the many neighborhood gangs. Like every other weekend, Ricardo took flight striking blows, ducking from bottles and stones. During each skirmish, there were threats and lots of blood on everyone's face, especially theirs. Ricardo took a hostage, dragged him to the entryway of a building, stripped him, kicked him a bunch of times, and then let him go dressed only in his underwear. We got home at dawn, but Ricardo went out again while I was sleeping. I didn't find out until the morning that they were operating on him.

"...so I tell you, my man, that I was getting bored, and then I remembered that I had two beers waiting for me in the refrigerator, so I decided to go home. I looked for my cigs, but I couldn't find them, and I thought that I had probably dropped them when I fled from the café. I felt better after I found my lighter in my jacket. I saw some kids ahead on the avenue, next to the houses. I thought they were trying to wash windshields for change, but then I noticed their clothing, you know, really fashionable, loose fitting, spanking-new basketball sneakers, hair shaven off. One of them started looking at me weird, and his friends started to do the same. I crossed the street to ask them for a cigarette, and while doing so I noticed some man looking over documents inside of his car parked next to the streetlight. When he noticed that I was approaching him, he closed his files and started the engine. When I passed by him, he stopped driving off. What you think?"

Ricardo was joining four other friends to buy some beers. He found himself face-to-face with one of his rivals from the previous night who ran away. He caught up to him, and his father as well, who was armed. Ricardo dared him to shoot.

The bullet entered the thorax, grazing the lungs, and then exited and lodged in his arm. Ricardo woke up a week later, when they were wheeling him from the intensive care unit to the recovery room. After two months, he escaped from the house of one of my sisters to go drink some beers with friends who wanted to celebrate his return to civilization.

Just then, it started to rain in the Bronx, and someone raised the volume on a stereo.

"...I decided to not ask them for anything. *Those fuckers are high,* I said to myself. I passed by them, alert, yet I didn't know what for. I heard a voice: 'What's up, faggot?' Twenty pesos, my jacket, and my lighter—that's all I had on me. Run. I never run away. I pretended I didn't hear a thing. Run. Too late. Fear's a drug that lets you go easily. 'Stop there and don't act stupid.' I stood against the fence, ready to throw some punches, knowing that no one there could survive one of my punches, but the little fuck stuck an automatic against my head. 'Empty your pockets,' he said here, in a low voice, like so no one would hear him. Three dumb-asses are more dangerous than a pistol, and I figured out that everything could happen very quickly, like some traffic accident that you don't end up surviving. The other two surrounded me. Their heads were stumps with bugged-out eyes about to pop. I didn't see anyone nearby. It's like we were floating alone beneath the stain of the yellow light from the lamp. One of them, with lips white from dried spit, threw a punch, but I ducked in time and it only grazed my face. The fucker laughed nervously before searching me. 'Relax, no problem,' I said, and showed them my money. The one holding a pistol snatched it from me and looked at the others in disbelief. He then asked for my jacket. 'Quick, and don't look at me, asshole,' he commanded while pressing the muzzle against my temple. One of the others kept on searching me, but he didn't find the lighter. I let them do it, but I was no longer scared. After that, everything happened at a slower pace. Cars passed by. Dogs barked. Footsteps in the distance. The dude with white lips couldn't stop spitting and staining the sidewalk with the soles of his Nikes, like he had some tick . . ."

A storm burst, and it splattered the suffocating studio. I got up to close the window, while Joe shouted that the tea was ready for Rose in the kitchen upstairs. Outside on the street, a sports car was slowly rolling down the street, rap music blaring, which momentarily drowned out the neighbor's music. The asphalt glistened like a knife's edge caressing a sharpener. I pretended to start cleaning up my studio so Rose would leave me alone, but she kept on talking, unable to pull me away from my memories.

Before Ricardo continued, I impulsively grabbed the bottle and nearly choked.

"...they kept on searching through my pockets, and that's when I pulled out my lighter and chucked it far away. 'What the fuck, you faggot?' I heard before the blow to the back of my neck knocked me against the wall. I came to my senses like Julio César Chávez during the last rounds. I was about to jump at the one carrying the pistol; they were some sad-ass motherfuckers, newbies, without the balls it takes to shoot. Trash for the evening news. But I remembered that time they put me in the hospital. I think that's why I was no longer scared: I knew they weren't going to kill me. I didn't want to lose my lighter, but the blow I received made me woozy. Life and death on auction. What bid would you place on them? 'Don't fuck with us because I will fuck your shit up,' said the guy with the pistol, now pressed against my forehead. The other ones kicked me so they wouldn't feel they were less badass. They trotted away from me and found my lighter. Fucking thieves dying of hunger. They tried to hide it, but they couldn't stop looking at me...they knew there was some fear within me, yet it would cost them a lot to find it. I asked myself if those fucking kids knew how much a Zippo cost. I walked to the metro and I felt entitled to jump over the turnstile and beg for money on the train. Nobody paid attention to my story. And you tell me, why would they sympathize? A few gave me some change, either from habit or from fear. I got to my room and it's like those thieves had figured out where I lived. I went to the fridge for a brew, and I cleaned up my room while my anger subsided. The worst thing is that that lighter brings back to mind a lot of good times . . ."

Me too, I thought, finally succeeding in getting Rose to go upstairs. I didn't dare tell her that I preferred looking out the window to her company.

Middle of March, I found an ad in the newspaper seeking peons to work at the Stanwich golf club in Greenwich. I spoke to Norma, and then I asked Michael to inquire about the position and check that the salary really was nine dollars an hour; I didn't want anyone to hear my accent over the phone. Moreover, Michael checked the country club out and gave me his opinion: "It's awesome, you could smoke pot it's so big, and the workers drive around in little carts." I didn't think about it much, and I packed my bags as soon as I arranged for an interview with the manager. Rose celebrated by buying herself some clothes. Upon saying good-bye, I promised her and Sandra dinner on me. It made me sad to know that Sandra was moving to Brooklyn, next to Coney Island. I would miss her discreet visits to my room to find out what I was writing. Sandra, my phantasmal neighbor, just like Liz Taylor in *Cat on a Hot Tin Roof*, standing in the open doorway, a glass of brandy in her hand, and her inseparable Graceland in her other arm. She never understood why I remained indifferent to her innuendos that we finish our awkward stretches of silence between drinks with sex. Shy and withdrawn like always, she would return to her chair to finish the night and her brandy by gazing out the window, accompanied by the music of Elvis and her cat. In the morning, she would put on her dark sunglasses before stepping outside to pay her share of loneliness among the inhabitants of Manhattan.

CHAPTER ELEVEN

Golf Course Maintenance at the Stanwich Golf Club

Every day I would wake up at five in the morning, still wiped out from work, and panicking that I would get to work late. The Stanwich Club had no tolerance for lateness or sick days, only efficiency and productivity, and that's why "we're number one in New England. *That's all that matters,* and because of that, those of us who work here put in our 110 percent, *always.*" That's how Scott the manager, wrapped up his presentation upon hiring me.

I showed up to the meeting because it sounded like an easy job. The help wanted ad specified only that one be in good health. I turned off the woodsy highway onto the paved driveway of the club. I drove Norma's car slowly, not trusting country-like stillness. I realized that if I were to work there I would need to buy a car and move nearby. Things were off to a bad start. While I tried to find directions to the main office, I turned off the radio, stunned by the impeccable courses beneath the noon sun, as impeccable as the distant houses hidden by the foliage, the lakes and artificial rivers lined by reeds.

The iridescent shadows cast by the pines trees and willows onto the windshield made it hard for me to see. I regretted that I had forgotten to bring my sunglasses. Butterflies in my stomach were about to make me pull a U-turn, go down the highway straight to the local library where old men fall asleep with magazines spread over their legs as they recline on La-Z-Boys facing the garden window.

It smelled of freshly mown grass. The silence seemed to hide some crime beneath curtains of different shades of green. At the end of the road I came across some clay and concrete tennis courts, empty. I turned to the right, looking for a spot in the stony parking lot in front of an area with huts. On the side, there was a fuel outlet with a black stain around it, and on the other side was a tool shed and tractors. I found a spot in between a Mercedes-Benz and a Jaguar.

I walked toward the main hut. Some workers in green uniforms were eating their lunches at a long folding table cluttered with sodas, sandwiches, fries, plastic lunch boxes, and caps. No one answered my greeting; they preferred to joke about the newcomer while they looked toward the manager's office, which had a large window next to the lockers. Next to the bathrooms there was a chalkboard with the names of gardeners and their daily duties written in a small and exacting hand.

It smelled of farm, sweat, and disinfectant. Above the microwave, a clock showed the time: 12:30. The gardeners finished their lunch, and then they got up in a hurry, heading off to their pruning tractors.

Greens, flats, fairways, tramps, all sorts of tools, heavy machinery, fertilizers, flowers, and seeds formed part of detailed instructions for performing incomprehensible tasks. I filled out the questionnaire, writing checkmarks and Xs in favor of myself, while the manager left the office to erase some instructions on the chalkboard and write new ones. Upon returning, he took his seat at the desk, and with a rough tone, he interrogated me about my immigration status, knowledge about gardening, and physical health. He had me in a corner; one mistake and the next sentence from his mouth would be "Maybe next year." I cloaked my ignorance by answering yes to everything, while Scott recited the demanding routine and the job's prison conditions.

The walls of the office were decorated with diplomas, trophies, and color photos of celebrities playing golf, some of them accompanied by the same touchy recruiter in front of me. Later in the interview, I made a jackass of myself by smiling at the warnings and the supposed fringe benefits of the job as if they were worthy of a standing ovation. It sounded like what I had heard in the past: prison terms based on envelopes with weekly checks. I was able to distract him a bit by asking about the club. "Yes, we organize a celebrity tournament, and this year Roger Staubach and Farrah Fawcett will be participating." The house on the grounds? "It's mine. I live there with my wife and my two children." I mentioned Ring Lardner and especially F. Scott Fitzgerald. "Have you ever read him? You have his name, as well as the name of the medicine I used to take as a kid. Hee hee. Fitz would have loved a membership on this other side of paradise . . ."

Lardner, the biggest writer of the Prohibition era, lived in luxury in Greenwich, and he was a close friend of Fitzgerald's and a role model for Ernest Hemingway and John Dos Passos. The Bell Syndicate would distribute his articles to 115 newspapers that paid him between $50,000 to $60,000 a year. Before he started writing, only Jack London earned as much with his prose. An agile narrator, he captured the banal spirit and superiority complex of the Lost Generation like no other writer in his time, as well as the typical North American during the early decades of the twentieth century. When they were neighbors in Great Neck, a Long Island suburb in New York, during a drinking binge Fitzgerald convinced Lardner to gather his stories into a collection: *How to Write Short Stories (with Samples).* Lardner thought up the title before falling asleep in the armchair on his porch. (Zelda Fitzgerald had dragged her husband to Great Neck, as he needed to write.

She knew very well that that meant money in the bank.) The critics exalted Lardner's cynicism and sense of humor in his depiction of the middle class.

But he was more extreme than they thought: he laughed at the entire United States, which in 1924 he described as an immense town of socially upward ranchers. Lardner and Fitzgerald respected each other deeply. They both liked good wine and liquor, and they knew a lot about the Gatsby-like world.

Fitzgerald and Dos Passos went looking for Lardner at his mansion in Greenwich. This was because Dos Passos, the youngest among them, said he admired Lardner. They had been drinking and it was dawn when they knocked on the door. Fitzgerald assured Dos Passos that there wouldn't be a problem and that they would find him awake; the unfortunate thing was that he didn't say in what state. One of the servants let them in and led them to the living room. There was Lardner like a mummy, seated on the sofa, his eyes wide open, but unable to pronounce a single word, wasted. What was Dos Passos thinking? That they would find him writing? Lardner was drunk as a skunk.

I preferred to digress while Scott scrutinized the application form with his yellow eyes, free from vices and reflecting a demented fervor for discipline. It was certain that his ancestors drank until they went crazy while hanging rebel slaves from trees, but Scott had altered his genetic disposition, and he had turned into someone as bland and efficient as the rye bagels and bottles of water he would consume during lunch break.

Scott was no better than us; he wasn't even bilingual. His demeanor as Mr. High-and-Mighty was the result of his degree, which he earned at the University of Rhode Island. He majored in golf course maintenance. That was a major for people with money living in the suburbs and who bought their clothing from L.L.Bean catalogs. After twenty years of giving orders, he was incapable of understanding the insults to his mother or the vulgarities that the Puerto Ricans would shout whenever his wife entered the break room, while she smiled and brought him lunch in a brown bag. She was as blond as he was, yet her hairs weren't burned and coarse from the sun like his. Scott had a photo on his desk of her and their two sons, all three of them wearing Bermuda shorts, ready to board a sailboat that was behind them. When she walked toward Scott's office, her beautiful thighs silenced any scandalous uproar, as she wore shorts and high-heeled sandals that clacked over the linoleum stained by work boots. She was a haughty Scandinavian beauty with tan skin and breasts larger than usual for a woman her size. She had small, hard thighs, like those of a man who has spent hours in a gym. We would have sacrificed anything just to bathe ourselves in her exquisite essence. To make her sweat while fucking her there on the table in front of everyone with the same merciless vigor that Scott used when assigning tasks.

Only the accountants at the IRS were interested in the numbers solicited by employers. The most they ever did while I worked at the club—no one had ever asked for my green card and Social Security number—was to send me a letter asking that I "correct the error" in the information I had provided. All the while, Uncle Sam took out taxes from my paycheck. By knowing the details of the job well, one could move about with relative ease. Scott was suspicious of me, as I had written down "reading" as my hobby on the job application; but it didn't matter in the end, as he still hired me. The reputation of Mexicans as untiring, loyal workers still had some value. Petty and continuous obstacles didn't leave one any more time than to think about earning as much money as possible. That mania is what helps one find tricks and strategies to handle heavy labor. I supposed that one needed to have some goals, but I couldn't figure mine out. I was fed up of living as a resident in that gulag, overwhelmed by activities full of conflict. An occasional fuck with some of the chicks that I would pick up around there was the only proof that the daily grind hadn't destroyed me completely.

Hell. After all, what's wrong with having several hundred dollars in your pocket each weekend?

On my very first day working I learned the origins of the other nine gardeners: three white Americans, five Puerto Ricans, and one more person, a Colombian, who had his papers in order. He was the newest employee, and he had been there for eight years. A sweetheart back in Medellín was still waiting for him. There was also another white guy, a mechanic, who was the butt of everyone's joke. Scott made him set up the traps for the skunks that made holes on the courses.

No one bothered to introduce himself. My name was written on the chalkboard above a list of tasks. For a week, Dimas, the old Puerto Rican, was in charge of training me, and he spoke to me in English and Spanish. He pronounced words in both languages as if he had food stuck in his throat. Scott would keep a close watch on us, and when he felt it necessary, he would call Dimas and give him instructions. Scott knew how to make himself present to show off his skills with the tools and machines, just like the instructional videos and manuals demonstrated.

The gringos were paid the best, and they had enviable livers: they would get drunk all day, starting in the morning. They spoke very little about themselves and always with brazenness and a bit of indifference. They were proud only about working more than the others and about being responsible for the special equipment. Cocaine made their gestures seem stiff and fake. When it was lunchtime, Steve would show off his collection of two thousand brand-new cotton shirts with logos. He would keep some wrapped in plastic in his trunk among half-empty bottles of vodka and dirty street clothes. He lived happily among us, drinking nonstop and breathing in the country air without anyone to bug him as long as he finished his job. A good portion of his salary went to alimony and betting. He kept a distance from his parents, who invited their distinguished friends to sip tea on the terrace of their country mansion in New Haven. Steve refused to work for them as a property administrator with a salary that would have been three times more than the one Stanwich paid him. Sometimes he was silent and at other times voicing his happiness about his life working outdoors; he preferred to wait for the inheritance while submitted himself to Scott's dictatorship.

After a few weeks I learned about an activity not written on the chalkboard: snort and drink on the sly while Scott drove around the club in a golf cart. On payday, we would hop into a car and drive to a small town nearby. Scott had made an arrangement with the managers at the bank to not ask for identification from the workers, just as long as we were wearing our uniforms. We would cash our checks before eating lunch in the parking lot of the liquor store on the other side of the highway. The gringos had some credit there. On Mondays, we would experience solidarity as a result of all being hungover. No one had money, and we would tell stories about getting drunk at home during the weekend.

The club was closed on Mondays. It was also the toughest day for us, as Sunday was our day off, and we would have to prune everything twice. It required absolute concentration to maneuver, for five hours straight, tractors with enormous collection bins and blades jutting out above the four tires. Beside the steering wheel, there were levers to go up and down and control the pruning. We would start with the narrowest areas. When it came to the fairways, we would trim in pairs, our vehicles going in opposite directions to give a two-toned look to the grass. Upon reaching the middle of our road, the morning fog would face us, riders astride monsters hungry for grass, ready to joust, straight out of nowhere. After every three sessions of cutting, we would have to empty the baskets full of grass into the bushes or alongside the paths.

On the greens, the duties were carried out on foot. The gist of it was to balance the weight of one's body after cutting to turn without stopping along the edges; to do this, you would have to turn with the lawnmower as if it were a heavyset dance partner. Before starting, we would have to throw away the holes made by the balls and shoe spikes with a type of two-pronged key. It was the slowest and most demanding task there. With Scott's approval, once we had cleaned, put away the tools, filled up the tractors with gas, as well as the chain saws and pruners, and once he gave a final inspection as we waited to clock out at 3:30, like kids itching to get out of school, sometimes we would stay in the storage room next door, where we would bet while throwing dice until nightfall. Winnings would be collected on payday: alcohol, cigarettes, or sandwiches. Everyone got drugs on his own and shared without making a fuss or mentioning how much he had spent on them. The foreman watched us from a distance, seated on an excavator, drinking whiskey from a flask and petting his Labrador, Rex. I liked to furtively study his hands and bleared eyes surrounded by crow's feet. The dude had various prizes in weight lifting.

Dimas told me that some years ago the foreman had been detained by the police as a suspect in the killing of his wife at their cabin, located in the Vermont mountains, where they would spend winters hunting. The detectives couldn't prove anything; he claimed that she had fallen from a boulder, drunk, after an argument. Sometimes he would smile while watching us; his teeth were as stained as the edges of an ashtray.

A black, sensual, and capricious beast whispered in our ears to never trust things and to keep her complacent and dissatisfied. She would show up while we spoke about the routine or if we dared investigate into each other's past and what brought us here. We would avoid questions with hoarse yet blunt voices, looking at each other like enemies during a truce, remembering that it was better to go from one sand trap to another, sweating, while others were trying to pit us against each other with metal razors.

The gringos were the same as their Hispanic coworkers, strong-willed and disobedient. I don't judge men by their actions or achievements. I simply weigh you with a very basic gut instinct: if I can trust you or not. It's an emotional gauge that instructs my interactions with others day by day. They either passed the test or they didn't. It was easier with women; we would just sleep together, and they didn't even have the chance to show me some of their gentler sides. They're so vain that they can't resist a new friend, yet they'll use their feminine wiles and coyness and make things impossible. I love loving them, but I never forget that I'm locked inside of a cage with a wild animal and that with each caress I'm running the risk of dying, ripped apart by her jaws. I didn't use medical pretexts or other issues about my health to work any less. I risked being fired or located by immigration if they asked for my Social Security card. As I was the newbie, Scott and the foreman gave me the toughest tasks. The other ones, due to their years on the job, had the right to choose. I abhorred all of them: the ones who were there before me and the ones who would be there after me...undocumented workers or not. But while the time passed, and as we trudged along ignoring each other, I would succumb to some of my hated obsessive habits, such as asking for overtime and counting the hours up each month to break my previous record; I looked at the mileage on the dashboard, and I would come up with shortcuts to save a few gallons of gas as well as time during the morning commute. Money tied me to the routine, making me become like the other ones, but worse, because I was the one who was always willing to turn my back on them when they wanted to include me in their condemned state.

I spent the first months digging ditches, taking care of sinking sand traps by myself, and sweeping and raking up leaves. I took my sweet time enjoying those routines. I spent hours alone on the grounds on a type of tractor. I squashed hundreds of mosquitoes against my neck, and I smoked out beehives, a task that left me looking like an inflatable monkey. I stopped my labor when I would notice the glint of sunlight on a bottle in the hand of one of the other gardeners. Then I would approach him to take a swig while he started on some insignificant conspiracy. By the tar-glazed ponds and the green and putrid rills, we would look for stray balls to sell to a supplier from city hall.

Twice a month I fumigated the ponds in a raft accompanied by Jim. He would row, going in a spiral from the center to the shore. I would put on gloves and a mask before starting the tank on my shoulder and the sprayer. It would spray a foul-smelling yellow liquid that made the water bubble. Jim liked putting on a mask of the Creature from the Black Lagoon and shouting nicknames and dares at the Puerto Ricans seated on their tractors by the shore. They, in return, would answer by fervently wishing for us to topple into the pond. The Puerto Ricans were hysterical and as untrustworthy as parrots.

Jim owed all of us money. He coaxed us two or three times to work with him in some gardens of local homes; he promised a chunk of change upon finishing.

Dimas had seen everyone grow old and dry up beneath the sun. He would always warn us about Jim. The old man was tough, and he had become bowlegged from so much work. He loved Scott as if he were an ungrateful son. For the past thirty years, he accepted that he would detest him during those moments when he asked for a raise, or when the gringos were chosen to do tasks that required heavy machinery. Dimas was our Virgil, always ready to point out the necessary details about the green hell.

Scott calculated the exact moment when I would be ready to desert out of exhaustion and boredom. Accompanied by Dimas, he took my garden spade and rake and assigned me to a pruning tractor, which I would maneuver with great skill, thanks to the old man's teaching. "There is no rest for the damned!" Gunter had often said. That phrase summed up our sentence to hard labor.

Scott supervised us each, one by one, by days and certain times. I would measure out his arrival from afar while I went over my duties in my head. Then I could receive him from my temporary dominions, ready to defend myself. Contrary to what I expected, Scott would smile, showing off his perfect pearly whites. After greeting me, he would look over his clipboard, checking details that were convenient to have at all hours: dates for future tournaments, what measures were taken to deal with skunks and opossum so that they wouldn't dig holes in the grass, cleaning and rolling the surface of the clay tennis court to keep it flat, directing and choosing the right lengths for pruning. Then he would take a deep breath and start talking to me about his liking the type of jazz you hear at shopping centers and running marathons. Everything in New York. Scott wasn't really talking to me but a higher-caliber listener, not this sunburned and sweating guy just pretending to listen so he could catch a few moments of not having to work, although later he would have to hurry to finish on time.

Scott bragged about his methodical process to become more and more refined, and how this had catapulted him from some small Midwest town, changing him into the unfailing manager of one of the most important golf courses in the United States. He had to narrate this to me, the only person he would see reading during lunch hour. The only one with 165 pounds of patience, who hadn't missed work in seven months, and who did just as much as the others who had been working there longer and had grown fat. The only one who didn't mock him, pretending to be speaking to others; the only one who hadn't been arrested for drunk driving, who hadn't argued with his wife in the parking lot about child support; the only who hadn't shouted "faggot" or "son of a bitch" in Spanish while he went from one end of the club to the other, assigning duties for the day. I had come to realize that Scott understood the insults mixed in with the verbal diarrhea that the other resentful ones spewed. On several occasions I saw him while he was shopping with his family on the main avenue in Greenwich, and I would dodge him. We could have submerged ourselves in a sea of shaving blades, fighting against the tide or simply letting ourselves be carried off by the force of a mutual enemy: monotony. If we didn't face this until the very end, the undercurrent dragged us to our lives here in the prosperous lands of New England, and we could aspire to pardoning each other.

$

A Salvadoran waiter at a diner in front of the train station in Greenwich told me about an opening for the night shift at one of the gas stations in town; it was the oldest and most prestigious one as it provided full service.

"Why don't you apply for it? You would earn more," I shot back.

"I don't like working outdoors and I eat for free here."

I immediately introduced myself to the manager, Mike. He checked about my getting hired with the mechanic and then with the owner over the phone. I found out later that they had called Gunter to get his recommendation. That very afternoon I took over the position that had once belonged to a Peruvian. Grin and bear it was in my genes, especially when it came to possibly earning up to $150 a day by pulling double shifts.

Working outside oxygenated my lungs, but it also provoked muscle aches and rheumatism, especially during winter. I was always on my feet. Upon getting home after midnight, I would make some coffee and have dinner alone in utter exhaustion, before peeling off my uniform and falling backward into bed. I would fall asleep faceup, stinking of gasoline, obsessing over little details having to do with my physical health and its dividends: twinges in my joints; the heater on high, especially during winter; noises from the street loud enough to be heard through the walls and shut windows; a poster of Cassius Clay raising his gloves after beating Sonny Liston; photos with inscriptions, all from well-intentioned women looking equally attractive and similar, good for jacking off to before falling asleep; piles of dirty laundry; a portable stereo and CDs never listened to; bottles of lecithin medication; unread books; an ATM card; a small desk with a portable typewriter in front of the window, next to a cork agenda board with an old to-do list.

$

All the houses looked like they were prefabricated according to instructions in *Popular Mechanics.* As soon as I got the job at the golf club, I had rented a room with an ample living room upholstered like a dentist's waiting room. The owner was an obese and short-tempered Irishwoman; once she called the police because my car was blocking the driveway.

The room was on the second floor, separated from the rest of the house by a staircase and door opening onto the first floor where the old woman lived, along with her husband and a fat, meddlesome dog with a skin condition. On the upper floor there was an entranceway and a kitchenette. I would go upstairs on tiptoes to avoid that fat busybody dressed in her blue bathrobe with embroidered flowers. She would pull herself up from the sofa, followed by her dog, and then she would rattle off the disturbances I had caused. The lapdog would bark and throw itself at my feet. The husband was a taciturn employee of the postal service; he had sunken yellow eyes, and he would greet me only at the end of each month when I would place the rent into his bony hands.

During summer weekends, that whale of a bitch flooded the backyard with her splashing in an inflatable tub, not giving a hoot that I would observe her from the window in the entranceway.

I had few visitors. I would ask them to remove their shoes before entering the house. We would spend the time hanging out on the carpet in my room, listening to music at a low volume on my CD player, speaking in whispers, careful to not give ourselves away to the fat landlady. I had learned a good trick from Michael and his friends. Inside the cardboard tube that once held paper towels, I would stuff some of the towels doused with fabric softener. We exhaled our cigarette smoke into the tube. The aromatic filter would work for up to ten cigarettes before it ended up looking like stained toilet paper. "This is the most ridiculous thing I've done in my life," a friend remarked while saying good-bye, stifling a marijuana-induced cackle as he walked down the stairs with his shoes in his hands.

I didn't wash my work uniforms. I even wore them on my day off. It seemed useless to worry about the way I looked after spending eighteen hours working at Stanwich and the Mobil station. There's no room for vanity with a schedule like that. I started showering on weekends after visiting one of the diners by the main highway, near the library. I would kill time at a table in front of the window. At the counter there were always men getting a buzz on the oily coffee—a cup cost you fifty cents, with endless refills—and they stared impatiently at the waitress. The women smoked light cigarettes, their lips stained with bile, and their hairdos seemed to have been combed with wood lacquer. Everyone scowled and sat alone. Once, the youngest woman I had ever seen there approached me at my table. I thought she had come to leave the check, but she wanted a cigarette and asked something. I said no at the same instant when, taken aback, she tried to pick up the pack. She remained standing and looked at me as if we had been friends for years. She obviously hoped that I would invite her to sit down.

"I went to the Salvation Army to look for a coffeemaker, but I couldn't find anything."

She sat down across from me and started to laugh, covering her mouth with the back of her hand. She didn't look me in the eyes. I thought that she was laughing at me.

"You look familiar."

"Everyone in this town should know me. I pump up to three thousand gallons of gas daily. I work at the gas station in Greenwich. And you?"

"Nothing much, just odd jobs here and there."

I asked for another coffee refill. The mood was perfect for having a drink, smoking one cigarette after another. I'm Mexican. She was "dying" to go to Acapulco. A probing conversation that didn't lack a *cómo se dice en español* and compliments about my shredded English.

"My name's Madison Marie."

"Are you from New Orleans?"

"No, hee hee."

She had the look and name of a whore from an Old West saloon. I asked if she had ever traveled to other countries. The farthest she had gone was to Baltimore and some town in Florida. She wore white sailor's pants, black high-heeled sandals that she left undone, and a turtleneck blouse with no sleeves and black and purple horizontal stripes. Her straight reddish hair reached her shoulders. She used lip gloss and eyeliner as blue as her eyes.

"I don't have a car," she said, before sipping her coffee.

"That's why I have never seen you. All of the cute girls stop at the station. I can give you a lift," I suggested, unable to take my gaze off her breasts, which bulged from the edges of her bra visible on the edges of her blouse.

"I live in Darien." That was ten miles up north. Then, while covering her cup with both of her hands, she said, "It would be great if you could give me a ride to the station."

Without being asked, the waitress tossed the check next to Madison Marie. I glanced angrily at the waitress, until I noticed a group of staring faces, as if they were waiting for the moment when we would start fucking on the table. "Get outta here or start the show," they seemed to be saying.

I paid at the cash register, feeling Madison Marie's breath on the nape of my neck. The owner of the diner looked at us gruffly from behind a plastic window as he handed back my change, and then he said something in Greek to one of the waitresses who approached a rotating dessert fountain. They laughed, ignoring us.

Parked on the outskirts of the train station, I insisted on taking her home.

"Another day, *gracias*." She gave me a long, hot kiss on the lips. She let me feel her up, and I suggested we go to my room.

"I told you already, some other day. I can't today." Then she laughed in the same way she did at the diner and asked me for twenty bucks. "I know that it seems like I'm taking advantage of your trust, but I'll take it as an advance payment. If you want me to go to your house, it will be thirty more. But in the car, it's only twenty bucks."

I looked for the crinkled bills in my pocket, and I took advantage of this to spend a moment arranging my wad of cash.

"How about next Friday night?" I said upon giving her the money. I searched in the glove compartment for a pad with receipts. I ripped out a sheet and jotted down my address and phone number. On the front, I circled the phone number of the gas station.

"You can find me every evening; I work till midnight," I said, voiding any excuses she might use that she couldn't reach me.

"Sure, no problem," and she gave me another equally passionate kiss and then gently squeezed me at the zipper as if she were concerned about being too rough with a little bird. Then she got out of the car and ran to the open-air platform. The train was arriving.

She called the gas station one Thursday afternoon a couple of weeks later. She had white and creamy skin, and her pubic hair was the color of maple leaves during autumn. When I kissed her, she gently sat in my lap. She smelled of soap and tobacco, and her cotton panties were fresh and thin. We smoked some weed in a pipe and then menthol cigarettes; we lit some incense, yet with the cardboard tube nearby. Stretched out on the carpet atop thick blankets, we looked at each other with glassy eyes, smiling like a couple of dummies. The giant landlady walked up and down the stairs, yet she didn't dare knock down the door. Madison Marie didn't like drinking and this made me feel like I was at a disadvantage. She never let me join her beyond the train station in Greenwich. Once she offered to introduce me to some of her friends in case she had to move someplace far away. I laughed at her good intentions. I never asked her anything important, because she never asked me anything either; our conversation was driven toward the exterior, nothing about the interior. We saw each other often until I told her that I was going to move. The excuse was the landlady. I said we should meet in a Howard Johnson, one that was near Norwalk, but she didn't want to and didn't explain why. When we said good-bye for the last time, I regretted moving in with Norma.

$

I agreed to split the expenses for an apartment again with my sister because it seemed convenient to join our salaries, save up some money, and leave the country as soon as possible. By luck, our schedules were different. She worked during the mornings as a Spanish tutor, and she cleaned houses during the afternoons, as well as taking surveys or being the nanny for neurotic and sad children. At home, Norma would keep herself entertained with the remote control while speaking long distance to her daughter or cleaning up the house. Sometimes we would get drunk on Saturday nights while playing cards with a guest. We lived out a variety of filial disownment where one would get oneself worked up with reproaches, schemes, and grueling paranoia. We couldn't love each other any other way. After her euphoric welcome when I arrived in the Bronx four years earlier, our relationship degenerated into endless quarrels and misunderstandings, nourished by our reality in a country where we were all strangers. If one of us had found out that the other one was addicted to a deadly drug or to a never-to-be-spoken-about perversion, our mutual appreciation wouldn't suffer as much as it did from that stingy and cowardly terrorism of low intensity, which was the product of tedium:

"Norma, the grocery list doesn't include meat."

"Spend more time at home and do it yourself."

"You'll hoard everything."

"The phone's getting expensive."

"I barely use it."

"You forgot to take out the trash."

"Where's my wine?"

"Tell that woman to stop calling you at dawn!"

"You should find someone to call *you*!"

"Loser!"

"Can you turn down the TV?"

There was no better incentive than *that* to work nonstop. We had become an incestuous version of the movie *The War of the Roses*. Norma made sure to control everything, and without saying it aloud, I allowed us to be bound to a country that she didn't like and that I considered to be full of imbeciles. Henry Miller was not mistaken: it was indeed *The Air-Conditioned Nightmare*. Dejection and monotony placed us by the doors opening to emptiness.

Norma was driven by the mission to "change me" as if she were a severe mentor to some licentious student. And thus, bit by bit, the upper floor on 60 Roosevelt Avenue, in the city of Stamford, became *her* apartment. *Brother, you can stay for as long as you wish. Just remember to behave as instructed.*

CHAPTER TWELVE

**In which...the Artist freezes...cruises Port Chester...
chauffeurs the lady and the midget.**

November. December. I had bought an '86 Toyota for $600
from a Canadian couple who were Gunter's neighbors. My job
at the golf club made it indispensable. For nine years they had
used it just for going to the supermarket and the train station,
which was only a mile from their home. The same route I
had covered on foot almost on a daily basis while working for
Gunter. During spring, the elderly couple grew violets, tulips,
and spikenards, as their Labrador caught up to them in age
while chasing butterflies and rodents. During the summer,
they would sip chilled wine on the porch of their enormous
house while lazing the day away on wicker chairs. They spent
their winters in the Bahamas.

I invested another $300 on new tires and some
adjustments to the engine. In the beginning, I was hoping to
change that small four-door with some snow and salt damage
into a showpiece—another one of my fantasies that I would
have to toss into the wastebasket on payday.

Norma and I lived a ten-minute drive from the town
center of Greenwich. By bus, the trip's duration depended on
the driver's mood. Elderly passengers, indigents, and servants
who had recently arrived in an area that had a concentration
of as much money as the budget for a Central American
republic. Our apartment was in an Italian neighborhood that

was being infiltrated by African Americans and Latinos. Some of the landlords were veterans; the majority were blue-collar workers and skilled laborers, and they were all embittered and strong believers in the death penalty. They would spend their Sundays getting drunk on cheap wine while taking care of their yards or cars, or while they grilled steaks.

I've always suffered from insomnia; it doesn't matter how tired I am. It's because of this that I have been able to read and keep a diary in which I almost always write about the same recurring obsession: to find out what keeps me from sleeping. Insomnia is a companion I wish I had never met. But its absence at night makes things uncomfortable; one gets used to the power it wields over one's actions. Windy nights especially keep me up. They get me up from bed, just like the dust and swirling leaves on the street. Sometimes I think it's a warning for me to keep in constant motion. The wind whistles and I hear the noises from outside that remind me of empty stomachs or indigestion, or hurried sex in some dark corner. What surprises me the most is the absence of any memories. It's as if I had been born that very day, beneath the sand-choked penumbra, and I can only imagine the activities of that very same day.

My whole life, I have avoided anything that poses an obstacle to my desire, which, as a result, means that they modify themselves to whatever poses least resistance. That's why people think I'm friendly and tolerant, when in reality I'm indifferent, and although I hate heavy work, it's an opportunity to not make any goals or defend my convictions, all two or three of them, which serve only to satisfy purely organic and contradictory urges, and always raise the suspicions of those around me. That's why insomnia is my dearest enemy: it keeps me on alert against sacrifices.

For weeks, I would doze while dreaming in intervals of a circular mountain chain amputating my toes. I would wipe off the blood with gasoline and a rag that I then used to cover the stubs. I lived beneath the white silence of Jack London, the Egyptian darkness of Mikhail Bulgakov, the white nights of Fyodor Dostoyevsky, and in Hans Ruesch's country of white shadows.

My nightmare first started on a Sunday morning. The area had been declared an emergency zone due to a storm that had been raging since Thursday. I put on two pairs of thermal underwear, socks, and a sweater beneath a thick coat, and I left for work. On the highway, yellow, red, and blue phantoms shimmered from behind the dense curtain of snow to warn of accidents and repairs. The trailers, like whales that had surfaced from the depths of the sea, passed me in silence, plunging into the icy darkness. There was neither sky nor land, and I crossed through that opaque and wide blanket while clutching to the steering wheel of my fragile, blizzard-shaken sled.

Tireless and punctual Fredson hadn't shown up at the gas station. It was a bad sign. We worked together fifteen hours a week. Fredson was the right-hand man for both Bob, the owner, and Mike. He did everything quickly and without gripes. He took care of the gas station as if it were his own, and he made sure that no one could compete with him. His obsession for duty was such that he even paid little attention to his own self. Bob said that was an example we should follow, and he encouraged us to come to the gas station during our time off to learn from his soldier.

Two rows of cars were waiting on either side of the pumps. I parked atop a hillock between two cars buried in snow. The front of my car jutted upward like a plane interrupted during takeoff. I jumped out from the Toyota, yelling at the drivers who were waiting. It wasn't even eight o'clock, and I still had to lift the pumps' switches and set up the temporary signs to the service station. The cars were honking anxiously and some of the drivers were cursing me. I had to turn on the halogen lamps.

I opened the cash register and I took out a hundred-dollar bill from beneath the money tray: it would serve as change while I started my shift. I placed bills and loose change in the trays outside and then I started filling up the tanks of the endless double row.

I went from one side of the service area to the other, manically working from the four pumps, charging and returning receipts. For six hours, it was only during snatches that I could go inside a couple of times for bottles of car fluids and extra invoices. I would take advantage of those moments to rub my thighs, remove my gloves and blow into my hands. In the past, the phone would insist on ringing with someone asking for an estimate or for a tow truck immediately. For now, it was silent. Outside, cars honking. Through rolled-down windows, the clients would shout out their demands for me to fill the tank, check the fluids and the tire pressure. Only a few handed me a tip. The older ones demanded absolute quickness and were shocked to see me alone. They possessed a deep-seated faith in their cars and SUVs with snow tires. How could they resist challenging the storm when they were snuggled beneath the blanket of their heaters and in powerful vehicles with lifelong warrantees? Where was Fredson? We all asked this to each other with the same motive, but with different feelings about his absence. Upon reporting accidents and road closures, the radios blasted that it was better to stay at home. *Fredson, you're one miserable and sneaky brother. Your pride reared its ugly head at the perfect time. You must be at home looking after your sickly mother.* My feet were stinging, I was itching all over, and I could barely grab at the change, credit cards, and receipts.

I spent that whole while debating whether I should send my obligations to hell. A sign hanging in the window said:

WE'RE OPEN ON SUNDAYS FROM 8 A.M. TO 10 P.M. By two thirty it had become dark and I decided to finish listening to my appeals. I was worn out and shivering. Without saying anything further, I put the nozzles in their places, I took money from the change box, and I entered the station in order to pull down the lever controlling the pumps. I locked myself inside with a key while I put away the change and stuffed the credit card receipts into an envelope to be placed inside the safe. Then I put the signs back inside the repair shop. I locked everything up, and I ran out to my car, ditching the drivers in the dark who were still awaiting their turns at the pumps.

I had problems getting the car started. Must've been the battery. I pulled the lever for the hood, and then I got out and started wiping dried acid from the wires. While I was doing this, some guy approached me to give me a piece of his mind. I ignored him, and he threatened to call Mike.

"Do whatever you want," I said while looking into the engine.

"I'll make sure that you don't have a job tomorrow."

"Fuck off."

"What did you say?"

"Exactly what you heard," I said while standing straight in front of him.

The guy returned to his car seething and telling everyone else about me. A hailstorm burned my face. The rows lurched off while shouting out curses that the storm swallowed. I cranked the ignition, and after some groans, the engine turned over. While the motor was warming, I scratched ice off the windshield and rear window with a spatula; then, with my hands, I shoveled snow from the rear tires. I got on the 95 and headed toward home. My nose was burning and, after a few miles, I started to yawn. *Bob, go fuck your mother. Fredson, fuck off, asshole. They'll pay me for the hours you missed. That, together with my pay, will come out to $150; not too bad for being* *frozen*. I drove slowly in the left lane, fearing that I would skid on a stretch of ice. Once again, a whale on wheels beneath the snow silently passed me.

I got off near the Stamford station and, turning to the left, beneath a bridge, the car started to rattle before shutting down. Enraged, I struck the steering wheel until the fear of being stranded made me respond. I breathed deeply, gazing through the windshield at dunes beaded with concrete stains. I felt sick to my stomach and as if I had low blood pressure. No way I could reach home on foot. There was something like a dozen streets too terrifying to walk down. I pumped some gas into the engine, and I cranked the ignition. After various attempts, the car, at last, turned over. And slowly, while leaning against the steering wheel and yawning uncontrollably, I reached home. I immediately went to the bathroom and turned on the hot water faucet in the tub. I stripped off my clothes. My skin was reddish, and the edges around my toenails were black and blue. I immersed myself, the water reaching my neck, and rested my head back against the tub's edge. That's how I stayed, dozing off to the rising vapors until I felt cold again.

I put on my thermal underwear and wool socks. The soft warmth against my feet made me feel sorry for my work boots, cracked from humidity and wear. I placed them beneath the heater, and it occurred to me that I should hold on to them to cast them in bronze like they do to baby shoes. I was hungry, but I was in no state to get up and cook. Stretched out on the sofa, I ate a few slices of ham with saltines, and then I fell asleep while watching a hockey game. Not too much longer after that, I called Estela, a Mexican friend who worked as a maid. Her bosses had left for a trip, so she decided to plan a party with other girls from the Latino guild. Without thinking about it, I dressed in front of the window. It had stopped snowing.

After some more struggles, I succeeded in turning on the car and I quickly reached a neighborhood with houses that looked like piers for yachts. I honked my horn to let them know I had arrived. The hostess opened the door and introduced me right after I crossed the threshold. Nothing but ugly chicks. They were listening to love songs. The furniture was slapped together from cheap wood, commonplace looking and not well taken care of. I did nothing but drink tequila and joke around until blacking out. From one drink to another, I collapsed into an armchair. At dawn, I awoke covered in my vomit, and I picked up a vase on the coffee table. It was filled with hard candy. I started to vomit again. I cleaned the vase, and I tried to remember what had happened during the night. Mad laughter, card games, stretching out on the carpet, absurd truth-or-dare moments. A fat dyke asked if I took drugs, because I sure looked like I did. I couldn't remember Estela or what I said to the one who asked that question. My body felt stiff and I was nauseated. My mouth tasted like metal, and my stomach was burning. The view outside the sliding glass door opening to the terrace depressed me. It was only two in the afternoon, yet it was already dark. I put on my jacket and wool cap, and while I was on my way to leave, Estela walked down the stairs; she looked pale, and her cheek was swollen. Totally wasted, she had fallen on the terrace and someone had helped her up to the master bedroom. She too had vomited on herself on the carpet. We couldn't figure out what time her friends had left.

"I've never seen you behave like that," she commented.

"Well, you don't throw too many parties" is how I responded.

We laughed like people always do when they're hungover and still not fully aware of their condition. The place stank like a barn. Estela went to the kitchen and returned with deodorizer. She sprayed it all over as if there were a swarm of flies. Now it smelled like a disinfected barn. I said good-bye, and the only additional thing that popped into my head to tell her was that if she started to feel horrible, she could call me, and we would drink it off in Port Chester. She didn't call me. But I'm certain she felt just as bad as I did for the rest of the day.

$

One Saturday, the buzzing from the refrigerator woke me up. It was almost noon and Norma had left for work. I stretched myself awake in front of the attic window where my room was located. The street looked like an accidental photograph. All of a sudden, a gust of wind sped off from the trees and snow-covered roofs in a vast whirl of leaves. Crows and seagulls flew over each other in daring plunges to hunt rodents or pick through trash heaped up by the bins.

There was nothing else to notice beneath the leaden dome of noon. A weak cloak of sunlight smeared against the snow like a rapist violating a woman who had passed out. The Toyota was parked out front, covered by ice. While neighbors shoveled snow from their parking lots, their children took advantage of the free time to chuck snowballs at each other.

Latinos and blacks started to outnumber the Italians who rented out basements and attics re-created as rentable living spaces. Our rents paid for the maintenance of those depressing "country-style homes" with frame-style roofs and useless chimneys, as all the houses came with gas heating. At the end of World War II, the Federal Housing Administration did what was right and gave ex-combatants and workers low-interest financing on mortgages with payments around $56 per month and $7,900 to pay in total after thirty years. The undertaking sought to repopulate the country and to encourage citizens to move into new areas.

From its very beginning, it created towns on the outskirts of the most important cities. Some arrivals to the new areas died before paying off their mortgages and passed on their debt to their children. A few among them paid off the loan and moved; the majority remained, stubbornly living on the good old times.

The landlords had seen their children and grandchildren grow, just like the credit they had earned at local community colleges, institutions, and businesses generations past. They rented rooms to us on shady conditions and at high rents. There were too many of us. We kept our dignity, yet they wouldn't trust us. They knew we could be rowdy, as long as we had the last laugh. And we were always fearful about the police or immigration agents.

Norma and I almost broke our lease while the ink was still fresh. Mr. Taglia raised the rent by $100 by using some mistake in the newspaper ad as a pretext. The oldest son consented that what the grumpy old man with a crick in his neck and a strong Tuscan accent said was true.

Black and Latino workers, undesirable renters, but ready to live by the highway and the interstate in a gloomy neighborhood surrounded by factories, warehouses, gas stations, and waste processing plants that attracted opossum, squirrels, and skunks. The streets were rarely traversed at night and, if so, only by people passing through and looking for drugs in the nearby ghettos, all located next to the train station. Our awareness that we lived in poor neighborhoods was consoled by the fact that the power and water always ran, the streets were paved, and that problems were taken care of quickly. The landlords asked for two months' rent in advance, for our work phone numbers, and that we try to minimize our accents. As a "favor," they wouldn't run the credit on the Social Security number on the copy of our bank statement. Norma and I had deposited $500 into our accounts long ago, and we had showed our student registration papers at the community college.

The Taglia family had sealed the front door. Like the rest of us, they had to enter the house from the rear. In order to reach our apartment, we had to circle the house, go beneath the stairwell belonging to the Taglias, and then go up another stairwell, one that was exposed, on the side of the property. Mr. Taglia and his two boys were plumbers and they loved working on their cars. Afternoons and on weekends, they entertained themselves by spending time in the driveway and repairing their cars and the work truck. They were always fighting. The old guy with his salty language was always babbling and pushing others. His wife, Doña Pola, would vociferate from her porch. Leaning against her balustrade, wearing an apron, drunk and deserted by her family, awaiting them with snot running from her nose while Norma and I would walk down on our way to work: *"Disgraziatos, tutti voi disgraziatos. My husband is a sonny bitch basket...Tutti. Porca miseria...Dey kill me!"* Doña Pola quivered her fat arms over her property, until her children and husband took her back inside, shouting all the while, but hidden from our view. They would shatter dishes, slam doors, and move furniture. We could clearly hear the snarling of the angry old man while he shut up his wife. Then he and his sons would set off in their truck, jabbering away. The "mama" would then sleep it off, snoring, before working the night shift as a nurse at the hospital.

The old man had installed a second oven beneath our bathroom. Doña Pola would prepare meals for everyone. Sunday mornings she would knock on the door. Norma would step outside to greet her as if that woman had taken care of her when she was young, and before exchanging hugs and complaints, Doña Pola, always proud, yet sorry about how much we worked, would hand Norma a salad bowl filled with warmed-up pasta. "Just *look* what she brought us!" Immediately, Doña Pola would gossip about the latest acts her troglodytes had committed. Upon leaving our presence, she would insist for us to not worry about paying the rent late. As soon as she closed the door, my sister would empty the pasta in a plastic bag, which she would later dump in the trash at night. On the last day of each month, Norma would go downstairs and promptly pay the rent before handing Doña Pola the salad bowl with leftover food from what we had made during the week, nicely arranged.

The raccoons grew nice and plump from this weekly exchange. The youngest of the Taglia clan would take care of them with a bat whenever he caught them stuck under the fence leading to the trash; he would put the dead animal in a plastic bag and then chuck it out his open window as he drove on the highway. The Taglia marriage had undergone years of intense fights in the United States. During one of the many domestic squabbles, Doña Pola began screaming as if she were being gang-raped by her family. A Guatemalan neighbor rapped on our door. She was scared and asked us to call 911 or go downstairs and calm down that rowdy bunch. I shook my head.

"Let 'em kill each other; it's not our business."

"But how can you think like that?"

"Well then, why don't you go and get involved in that mess."

Before finishing our argument just like the Taglias, I convinced her to go home, but not before asking her if she had her papers in order.

"Not yet."

"Is that what you're going to say when you have to go testify?"

Norma finally agreed with me.

$

It was my first free Saturday in months, so I was able to stretch out in bed and finish reading a book on the Renaissance. The Borgias had a great life. Next to me, I had an English dictionary, notes, tobacco to savor, and wine. I fell asleep and I awoke in the evening, my palate dry, and in a restless mood. After finishing the golf season at the club, I was able to handle my schedule at the gas station, and I even raised it from seven to ten hours a day, not counting voluntary overtime. As it was the weekend, I finished a bottle of red wine (I later changed my preferred label to another after seeing that it was the same one that made the Taglias lose their minds). Then I tidied up my room, wolfed down some food, listened to the weather forecast, and shoveled snow while speculating on the right moment to leave the country.

I refused to start the application process for my legal residency despite the abundance of shysters who specialized in that racket. The process could take years and required $5,000 and the desperate search for some employer who would plea for my case in front of an immigration officer. Another alternative, which was shorter and simpler, was to marry someone who was a citizen—they were almost always of Puerto Rican origin—and pay her a fee running up into the thousands. No thanks.

Europe sounded great.

My journal was filled with sums and average spending. Once in a while I would send an article to the cultural supplements in Mexican newspapers. At that time, I didn't know what happened to those pieces. Some years later, I found out that they had indeed been published in the major newspapers of Mexico City while I was looking through newspaper archives. I never received a cent for my articles, no, not from that horde of unhappy souls that comprise the editors of newspapers.

Before midnight falls, you think that you'll have some energy for the hustle and bustle and to be creative enough to have even more; but after finishing your shift, your body shuts down, lazy about getting to the girlie bars and whorehouses. After midnight is when those dark and treacherous avenues weigh on you even more. But there will always be something there to make you feel better, more alive and proud that work didn't screw up your day.

As in a funhouse with mirrors, I saw myself reflected in other laborers. Boxed in, no guarantees about anything, trying to hide their third-class status with nervous glances and broken English. Our cars also demanded a lot from us. Some of us spent scandalous amounts of money on them, for example, the mechanics at the gas station. They were Antillean Casanovas driving the latest model, always waxed and the engine potent. They would cruise slowly, calling out to girls and accumulating miles on the speedometer as well as nasty looks from blondes. I trusted my Toyota.

$

My throat was dry from the heater. Driving down deserted streets would relax me as I made my way to a barstool where the snowy night would become less tedious. I covered myself up with winter clothes, and while making my way to my Toyota, I looked at the thermometer outside the Taglias' door: fifteen below.

The key was to not stay screwed down in the same spot. Wasting time and ruminating are activities that you face during heated soliloquies. That's what made one woodcutter start shouting from the end of the bar, aching to talk to someone after a day of chopping trees that had been felled by the storms. But talk to whom? What the clients least wanted to hear was the same ideas from the mouth of an enraged Pole From behind the bar, Harry offered darts, pinball, happy hour, horse betting, sports on the television screen, and hard rock. Everything at once.

But Harry wasn't a procurer for everything. The mutton-fisted Pole with muddy boots would have to sit still in front of his beer and reconsider what was still lacking. A salary paid for electronic junk, a Social Security and green card (both fakes), used cars, clothing, alcohol, drugs, CDs, fast food from around the world, porn, some money to send back home, bets, massage parlors, even donations to the church, night school for barely literate adults, trips to the casinos in Atlantic City. Everything in reach, except when we were done going down the list, we were still desperately looking for a woman.

$

Driving on sleet and frozen puddles provokes unease, like in those indescribable yet always gloomy dreams. It must be because they expose us to desires hidden among frustrations. Insomnia is like a dripping leak in the soul. Behind me, a police car was following me and looking up my license plate on their radio. They let me go. Pedestrians don't exist in an area with no public transportation after six P.M. To go to another town, you would have to travel through numerous streets before reaching cold and abandoned train stations and resigning yourself to an interminable wait before the next train arrived.

The loudspeakers announced the itineraries and train routes like announcers at the horse tracks. On holidays and weekends, the waiting area at the Stamford station would fill up with weird sorts like lost souls wandering among the cleaning staff and the few evening travelers. The panhandlers would take naps in the bathrooms and in the waiting area booths, but when the train arrived they would go to the platform to beg and to snatch up newspapers and leftover food destined for the trash cans. The vibration of drums and bass announced the arrival of coaches operated by defiant blacks.

No family, no visits to church, not even meetings with immigrant associations, or other groups for athletes, addicts, activists, or intellectuals, nothing. My only company: cigarettes, analgesics, dietary supplements, drugs, wine from a jug, and a watch I won as a prize for my performance at Stanwich. The United States. Territory belonging to a foreign legion that makes superhuman efforts to never be abandoned.

At a red light, I observed the thick gray clouds rolling quickly, fleeing the ocean. There were small snow mounds on the sidewalks. I placed my frozen hands under my thighs; the snow would quickly bury the hope for a new sunrise.

The landscape reminded me of Mexico City on those hungover New Year days. I had half a tank of gas left to burn on those steely and icy streets. I kept myself entertained by riding alongside cars and then passing them without putting on my signals. There's something arousing about the pendulum of fear when you're unable to perceive the effects provoked in the other.

A beam of crepuscular acetylene floated in the south over Port Chester, the little Tijuana between the state of New York and Greenwich, Connecticut. That's where we would go to have fun until dawn. It was the only town nearby where you could get beers at the supermarket after seven at night and on Sundays. In that twilight zone there were no prohibitions against smokers, and the racial mix in bars and dance clubs was tolerated in an agreeable way.

The shop signs and billboards on Main Street reflected the influx of Latin Americans. SPANISH SPOKEN. TEMPLE OF ALL THE SAINTS. MONEY WIRED TO ALL PARTS OF SOUTH AMERICA. THE INCA, TACOS DON PEDRO, ¡VIVA MÉXICO!, SANTO DOMINGUITO, AND RINCONCITO CALEÑO. The fellow countrymen walked about peacefully in their thick winter coats, cowboy hats and baseball caps. Fresh from the shower, they would smile on the avenue, showing off their gold fillings.

The seasonal jobs had ended, and many workers were ready to spend the end of winter with their families, thousands of miles to the south. I remembered how, as a child, I would anxiously await the gifts that my father would send with his friends from Rosenberg, Texas. During those years when he lived there, he never visited us during Christmas. He preferred to visit us during the summer; he would come home with wads of dollars and a nostalgia that would vent itself out in wild parties where my mother would sing boleros. The entire family would get together, and at the start of autumn, we would say good-bye to our father at the airport; he was always accompanied by various workers he had recruited.

I parked the car. I stuffed my leather-and-wool gloves in my jacket, and I got out, smoking while I walked. The options consisted of three bars for whites, three Hispanic dance clubs, and a topless joint: CHICKS & DRINKS ALL NIGHT LONG! All were close to the train station downtown. A neon-green stripper crackled while suspended in the black sky. On Main, there was a twenty-four-hour diner that filled up with day laborers, drug addicts, and rock 'n' rollers who would dress up like they came straight out of *The Wild One*. On the walls, there were autographed studio photos of musicians who had once waited for fame in those plastic booths with cushioned red seats. Behind the counter was an enormous and filthy bar; a neon border in red and blue ran along the upper part of the bar. The black-and-white images of the old luminaries were reflected there. The diner was a supernatural collage of epochs, faces, and proud stances taken from the Americans' triumph against the Nazis, their triumph in Korea, and their martyrdom in Vietnam. The clients preferred to sit at the tables. At the bar, someone was leaning over his drink, as if waiting for the perfect moment to plunge.

I never asked for more sophisticated places, designer drugs, fading lights, or nymphos and crooked dandies. The characters from my experiences would rise up here and there, spinning hidden along the orbit of my obsessions, reluctant about suddenly revealing themselves. They were burlesque, and I would challenge myself by trying to rip them from the shell of my lonesome wandering, but I would have to satisfy myself with mere scraps.

The Ramones and then Los Tigres del Norte on the following night had played at the theater in Port Chester as part of their respective tours. Inside of Chicks & Drinks, the hostesses and strippers—who were made up of blacks, Eastern Europeans, Asians, and Latinas—spread out among the clientele who were all from the same origins.

After eating a hamburger, I walked out to the street and headed off toward a bar called the Beat as if the woman of my dreams was waiting for me there.

Some heat entered me on the second drink, and it made me think of Rebeca. It would be difficult to get her to come out. Even more difficult, as this was about having some cheap whiskey. Apart from the fact that she didn't drink, I didn't know much about her, or at least not enough to grasp the cause of her incurable case of melancholy. We met each other at night school while I sought out a booth in the library where I could catch some shut-eye before my class started. She greeted me in Spanish, we talked nonsense, and she struck me as timid, but she laughed at my accent from the capital, and she advised me to get rid of the tattoos on my arm. "You might have some problems finding a job," she noted. We exchanged phone numbers, and she set off quickly for her classroom. She was a student majoring in education, taking her advanced level classes. I couldn't pass advanced English. Despite that one initial encounter, she would leave me sporadic messages that I would never answer. Norma answered the phone on several occasions, and they became fast friends. One evening, she called me at the gas station, and she asked if she could call at dawn, after I got home from work. I said yes, thinking she would never call me. But I was wrong. That's how we would get together, always after a week of hot and heavy phone conversations, in order to act out the very things that kept our ears glued to our receivers.

Slowly but surely, I became attracted to her morbid self-sacrifices, especially when it came to work. But basically that's how all of us, the undocumented, behaved. Apart from speaking French and Berber, Rebeca was interested in learning Spanish, and she was able to do so with ease. She paid for her degree waiting tables at a Tex-Mex restaurant where lots of Mexicans worked. She had been unfaithful to her fiancé ten years past when they were in Morocco. To save her honor, as well as that of the two families, she had to beg for forgiveness on her knees. In the end, it was all about money; her family had some, but his didn't. They solved everything by offering a fabulous sum to the offended and granting the groom full control over his wife and her finances. The locals never heard about the scandal and they celebrated the religious ceremony, but both families agreed that it was best for them to go far away. Rebeca remained the adulteress, condemned to be so here and there, without access to any religious pardon, hounded by guilt and the jealousy of her husband, who was also a waiter as well as an adulterer, just like her, but with Polish women and other Moroccan immigrants.

Anxiety ate at Rebeca while we spent evenings and nights in nearby motels. Sometimes we would talk about our lives. It was very difficult to get her to smile. I told her not to hold back on doing so and that everything I told her had a moral to it. When we would say good-bye, my legs could barely keep me up. Just like myself, Rebeca barely slept, but only because she was convinced that one midday siesta was enough for her. I never saw her brush her teeth or get sick during the months that we had our supposedly secrets trysts; however, her bittersweet odor resulting from hard work, submission, and guilty pleasure crushed all of my paranoia.

There was one time when I waited for her for quite a while at the bar inside the restaurant where she worked. I asked for another beer that I didn't enjoy, as I was fed up with the bartender's poor service. The Tex-Mex place was decorated like some cantina from the Old West for haute couture cowboys. There were no Latinos tending the bar or waiting on tables, but there were plenty in the kitchen. Two elegant black men wearing glasses were sharing some drinks and whispering at their small table, which faced the window with its view of the iron bridge where the train would pass. The bar was the perfect spot for white women who wanted to hook up. Perhaps that's why the bartender rolled his eyes when he saw me. I had the complexion of someone who might ask him about a job at any moment. Rebeca got along well with the folks working in the kitchen. With her limited Spanish, she made them believe that her parents were from Mexico. Rebeca was classy, despite her corpulence. I always felt the urge to pinch her, but I never did so. I preferred to trace the folds of flesh when she was naked. She had an enormous birthmark on one side of her hip. As far as I was concerned, that sign, along with her Velázquez-like plumpness, served as evidence of her sexual gluttony, which she punished with a profound fatalism that comforted her. I told that to her when she once made some scathing allusions to her rolls of flesh. We busted up laughing. At last, she had let herself laugh.

Nos vamos? That was her question each time we met up. In the tone of her voice one could detect lasciviousness, as well as a fear of Jalil. Danger made us all the hornier. We would go in my car, and then we would return for her car in the restaurant's parking lot. I would answer her questions about my life in Mexico and the States while we were on the road. *I will tell you what I want to, what I remember, what you won't ask more questions about,* I would think before responding. "I have no time nor am I in the mood for the nostalgia and lunch-break sentimentalism that you hear from the men working in the kitchen. I too was like that," I said aloud. And it was an icy January. I turned onto the highway, and all along the way to the hotel Rebeca would look to make sure that her Othello wasn't following us.

Even though she was separated from him, we seemed like two fugitives, and Rebeca, in keeping with her absolute abandon to being a slave to lascivious regrets, would confirm my suspicions about her two-timing with the most unexpected phone calls. "Now you're my man," she would murmur sweetly into the receiver, "and you're free to do to me all the things you fantasize about." I looked at a phone booth in an area near the bar, and I repeated her phone number to myself.

All of a sudden there surged forth a scandalous group of adolescent punks, just as amusing as my daily shift at the gas station. The barmaid looked like a Mennonite with her overalls, and it seemed as if she had cleaned the glasses with her greasy, uncombed hair. She moved about restlessly, perhaps to underplay her own drunkenness and to make sure that no one left without paying for the multicolored drinks that lined the counter. Four fellow countrymen of mine hesitated to enter the bar. They lurched at the entrance, as if deciding between getting drunk at the Latino clubs on the corner or getting drunk among the cooler shoving and pogoing next to the window, where the glint of neon from a hanging advertisement cast upon them greenish halos like they were idols upon an altar. The bravest among them decided to enter for a beer, and he was quickly followed by the others. They looked around with vivacious glances. We recognized each other without having to state where we were from. We kept our distance.

Shortly thereafter, I left for the Willows. It had more space. The most important local bands played on its stage. By the time I reached it, the main hall had turned into a crowded sauna brimming over with alcoholic euphoria. After the live show, a lot of single girls arrived, attracted to the series of Japanese anime porno playing on the jumbo screens.

I bumped into a few people I knew: busboys, waiters, and deliverymen. They tried picking up on girls from back home, yet the girls would snub them and try to get the attention of gringos. They could hold off for months before deciding to offer the magical realism of their favors with hopes for a legal residency. Moreover, they were in competition with the gringas, who were more soused and slutty. I greeted my acquaintances, and they greeted me, and I kept on, slipping from their gripes about salaries, injustice, or racism or their endless nostalgia for our marvelous and warm countries. There were some Moroccans, always sober, dark rings under their eyes, skinny, and dressed like cheap accountants. It was easy to recognize them; they stared unabashedly, and they erupted in guffaws whenever a woman passed near them. There we all were, bent on hooking up by using our *Inglés sin barreras*. The gringo had more hope, even in clubs where there was no wait list. It was a distraction from his university studies or from the office were he worked; for the rest, being in one of those places meant sweating the energy that had been stored up for the next day's grind, which was impatiently awaiting them.

After two in the morning, the place started to empty out and I thought it was the right time to return home and not get stopped by the cops for driving shit-faced. The last time I got caught, I had to pay $150 after pleading guilty in front of the judge. My court date was sent to me in the mail. The courtroom was filled with the poor and needy and other types well versed in committing misdemeanors. We were the chump change filling up the cash register.

During the deafening after-hours at dawn in the Willows, the music spun by the DJs impeded all polite chatter with those next to you, which usually consisted of an adolescent joking about getting past the bouncer with a fake ID or having passed for an adult. I took one more drink for the road, and then I stepped outside to sober up by walking in the snow. Upon reaching the end of the road that ran into the main avenue, I came across some drunkards huddled inside the doorways of warehouses because of the cold. Behind me, I heard someone trying to get my attention; I turned around and saw a group of blacks walking together in close formation. *"Hey you! Wait a second."* Beneath the misty light, they looked like a horde of monstrous Eskimos spitting smoke. While they paused to smoke their pipes, I quickened my pace, taking care to maintain my balance and not slip on the traps of frozen water. I passed beneath the iron bridge that the Metro North train uses. When I reached the corner, I stopped. No one was coming after me. *They're not looking for you, relax, you coward, and you better think twice before you come to punk out in Port Chester.* On the avenue, a cop car slowly patrolled. Some gringos were rushing on foot to the nearby train station.

I headed toward the diner. I rejected several offers to share a beer with the street drunks; I remembered seeing some of them sober when I first reached the town. I sat at the bar and ordered a Coke while studying the photos of musicians dressed up like pimps. I lit a cigarette and eavesdropped on the chatter taking place between two guys at a table close by. One of them was trying to convince the other to walk to a nearby whorehouse. They looked like a Dick and Perry straight from Holcomb, fugitives worthy of *In Cold Blood*, and they made the few clients, who were eating in silence, feel uneasy. But they especially unnerved the one waiter who was also in charge of the bar, as they would roughly call him over every so often for another refill of coffee. Dick got up to use the bathroom twice, and he would slowly walk back to his spot, as if giving us the opportunity to admire his six-foot-five stature while he complained that there was only cold water coming from the bathroom sink faucet. Upon reaching his booth, he settled in next to his friend. Unbathed and sour-faced, they smoked and avoided looking at each other. All of a sudden, Perry gruffly looked over his shoulder at the street, as if sensing that something wrong was going on outside. Both of them had blurry tattoos on their fingers. They seemed to be unable to relax after having sold their jalopy Chevrolet. According to Dick, all they needed to do was knock on a window and ask to come inside. It wasn't a place that was open to just anyone; the clients knew about it from word of mouth. I remembered the location; you had to turn left on a street at the end of the avenue heading north. It was in a mixed neighborhood with mechanic shops for motorboats. "We've got nothing to lose," Dick insisted, "it's that easy to get inside the whorehouse." He was blond and well built; his hair was combed back and he wore a coat. Perry had bushy eyebrows, and he was dark and taciturn, and he wore an army coat and jeans that were several sizes too large, frayed at their cuffs, which covered his crippled boots with torn points that stuck out from the edge of the booth where he rested his legs.

The parking lot was a lunar landscape. I brushed snow off from the windshield before starting the car. It fired up without a problem, no rattles, no desperate pumping of the accelerator. Nothing to fear, despite the engine stalling from time to time; I felt satisfied with the daily maintenance that I did at the station, under the guidance of the black mechanics who worked the morning shift. To avoid skidding, I followed the trails on the asphalt left by other tires. Several blocks later, I passed by an Anglican church, and I braked at a red light. Behind one of the parked cars, there was a woman clutching an enormous paper bag; it seemed like she was looking for something, as she moved her head from right to left and stood on her toes.

Taxis were available with a phone call, and the telephone booth was nearby and empty. I started to move. In the rearview mirror, I saw a cloud of smoke ascending in a quick spiral because of the icy wind. The woman stepped off the sidewalk and briefly studied me before approaching the passenger-side window, getting my attention with a bony hand. I leaned over to lift the door handle. The old woman looked like she had recently spent the night at a homeless shelter.

"Can you give me a lift to High Ridge Road? It's not too far. I'll pay you."

I spent a moment looking at the asphalt silvery with sleet; I tried to utter some excuse as to why I couldn't do so, but the woman was opening the door. The drivers behind me started honking their horns, as there was a cop car at the end of the row of cars. I decided with a "Let's go."

She took forever to get inside the car, despite the fact that the paper bag was a cinch to move. It was my opinion that she wasn't carrying anything important, perhaps some cookies or cat food. With ease and calm movements, she let it be known that she didn't wish to look at me once she was in her seat. She was dwarfed by her enormous black wool overcoat, which was buttoned up to her neck; it was frayed, but expensive. Her blond hair was natural, yet greasy. She was fortysomething. Without paying attention to the road, she rummaged through her bag as if that's where she kept her manners hidden and she was trying to find the rudest ones available for traveling with a stranger. She gave me a headache, and I cracked open the window to air out the stench of alcohol.

High Ridge was on the other side of town, up north, a thirty-minute drive if traveling at 60 miles per hour. It was a zone where retirees and office workers lived—desolate, especially during the humid and stifling summers. I had spent some time there with Jim, sweeping dried leaves from gardens or shoveling snow from the driveways. It was also one of my ways to get to the golf club.

Everything there is symmetrical. The risk of getting lost down dark lanes always ends with a return lane for U-turns. A driver needs only to follow the route that leads to the main highway or the turnpike, where every five miles there is a lane starting exactly one mile before it exits to a town. Spectacular fluorescent signs seem to cut the misty curtain of the horizon. Among the signs announcing towns, routes, gas stations, motels, and malls, the golden arches of McDonald's are the most numerous. Paranoia resulting from the Cold War planned the turnpikes. They subjected the countryside's monotony to the rigidity of Fordism. If legendary diners on decaying routes still earn some marginal notes, they're an obsolete presence in a country that reinvents its past through highways. Nothing changes in a panorama designed to remain as a monument to efficiency. One elm tree is like the next one. A Getty gas station is the same as a Mobil, which is the same as a Texaco or a Sunoco. A McDonald's is the same as a Burger King, which is the same as a Wendy's. The same, the same, the same. There's no room for exuberance. My thoughts, at least, went from normal to unpredictable without apparent risks. Life is a highway with a speed limit, and I was driving in the fast lane in an old car with worn brakes.

"I believe I know you. Don't you work at Bob's service station?"

"Yes, but I'm sorry to say that I don't remember you."

"It doesn't matter, I rarely go there. I don't drive, can you believe that? I'm very nervous. When you get to the Sunoco, turn to the right, go up the hill to where it ends; I live at eleven-forty-eight."

How did she know about the Mobil station? Did she go there with someone else? Was she part of Mike's family? Was she spying on me? Menopause made her trust in a stranger. We were traveling at 70 miles per hour on a junction to the Interstate 1, headed toward Boston. I quickly glanced at her shoes with bands and buckles, stained by salt, and the bottom buttons of her jacket, open, revealing part of her light wool dress that showed the shape of her thighs, which were open and not wearing stockings. Her voice would break, as if it were emitted with radio static. I tried to touch her leg while shifting gears, but I brushed only against her overcoat. I shifted into fourth gear like taxi drivers from Mexico City when the passenger bugs them: I pulled on the stick shift as if I wanted to stab it into one of the rear tires. I asked myself if it was her anxiety that impeded her from driving...this woman who smelled of blankets and rancid perfume. Even the most subnormal people in Connecticut had their license. All sorts of freaks pulled into the Mobil station. I looked at her, seeking out her eyes, and I discovered an enormous birthmark with hairs beneath her ear. The broad seemed like some sleepwalker, gazing beyond the dark firmament cut in two by the fluorescent stripes of the road.

When we crossed a town, the old woman tried to look out the window at the stores. Ladies and gentlemen! Boy and girls! Here, on the border of any highway, we have people whose age, income, number of children, problems, habits, conversations, attire, possessions, manias, perversions, and even blood type are similar! All of them engendered by a blind fanaticism to order, breast-fed by a never-seen-before greed, one that is insatiable and lecherous and that has turned its women into industrious consumers of cheap products, who see their time as serving only to cart their children around in pricey cars that are all the same, even when it comes to their air fresheners. These little ladies of virginal appearance— with ample sexual experience out of wedlock, with shameful appetites—they have their radars set to detect what others consume, and with salaries that you all, my dear friends living on miserable wages (and of course I include myself among you, hee hee), well, we could get along for years on that amount without ever bothering anyone, for many years without any worries, even in this fucking winter climate...!

After a while, I reached the end of a narrow and woodsy lane that came to a fork. I turned to the right. The only odd thing about the house with the address of 1148 was how, unlike the other homes, it had enormous black trash bags—like the ones seen at night in Manhattan—in front of its unpruned bushes. The glint in the eyes of raccoons, like marbles, betrayed their location, while they prowled near the trees and the trash bags. The aging broad scratched her nose and made no indication since I braked that she was getting out of the car. I feigned indifference and waited for the pay she had promised me. I gazed into the emptiness and imagined the woman in her youth. *Okay, Bette Davis, kiss me or get out, I don't have time for games.* But I now had "Baby Jane" pretending that she was still young. I remembered acquaintances taking pictures of themselves while they leaned against the cars or stood in front of the homes of their bosses, and how they would send them back home like postcards for their family. *Come! Come!*

The old broad remained in her seat, lost in thought. It was time for me to remind her why we were here.

"Lady, I gotta go." I was almost begging, yet I didn't know why.

"Which way are you headed?"

"The same way I came from."

"Okay, well, then just wait for one bit, and I'll go back with you."

With the agility of a ferret, she got out of the car. She set off running toward the trash bags as if she were going to leap onto them, and then she dashed into the house. She opened the door without using keys and turned on the porch lights from the entryway. I started smoking just like Dustin Hoffman in *Straw Dogs*. To take her back would mean that I could double the price. I took advantage of her absence to do a U-turn. I turned off the motor and I waited. I don't know for how long, but I waited until the last houselights had been swallowed by the night.

$

I saw her approaching from the rearview mirror. She was lugging an enormous cardboard box, assisted by a midget who was dressed up as if he were about to set sail on a whaler. Behind her, another woman was approaching, just as old, but with rabbit teeth. I started the car, turned on the lights, and looked out the window to see how many cigarette butts had accumulated by the front tire. Five. I was ready to drive off as soon as they paid me, but the midget had already opened the rear door. He was panting. Without saying a thing, and with the arrogance of Captain Ahab, he got into the car and vigorously placed the box next to himself.

"No, no, no, just wait one moment. Get that box out of here."

"I'm sorry, bud, but tell her yourself; it's not my problem."

I felt the urge to strangle him for having answered me like that straight to my face. I got out of the car.

"Lady, I believe we have a misunderstanding here. Call a taxi."

"There's nothing you can do, you're already here; you can drive away but you'll be bringing him with you as well as the box, and I won't pay you."

She stared at me with a watery and reproachful gaze, the type of gaze that old maids use with men. Then she turned around to kiss the other woman on the check and sat down with an air of entitlement next to the midget. He rested his arm on top of the box and panted triumphantly.

"Nothing bad will happen and I will pay you double. Doesn't that sound good?" Baby Jane said while she cracked open the window.

I looked at both of them; proud, they took each other's hand, exuding faith. The broad had bathed herself in perfume and put on red lipstick. I got back into the car and started the engine. The road seemed abandoned and difficult to navigate.

"When you get to the avenue, you'll turn to the left," said Ahab, as if guiding his ship against Moby-Dick. He wore a peacoat buttoned up to his chin and wool pants. He spoke quickly and with his tongue stuck to the roof of his mouth. The old woman sat in silence impassively, looking straight ahead. The midget began to tap a quick and monotonous beat on the box.

"Turn here," the old woman said.

"This isn't the main avenue," I replied.

"It doesn't matter," the midget said.

"I wasn't talking to you," I responded with anger, making a sharp turn. Ahab snapped his mouth shut, and for a flash, we stared at each other sullenly in the rearview mirror. I drove down a road with gray bushes that hid the opposite side of the road. In the mirror, I saw that the old woman was looking through the box.

"Just where are you headed?"

"Keep on going straight, and don't worry about it," he answered, keeping his eyes on the road.

We entered a small town far from the highway. The only lights on were at the fire station and a few Christmas trees inside of stores.

I stepped on the gas and zipped past caution signals and red lights. They didn't say anything. If a patrol car stopped me, they would have much more explaining to do than I.

"What's your name?" I asked the midget while looking at him in the rearview mirror.

"They call me Charley," he gruffly responded.

"And yours?"

But the old woman pretended that she didn't hear me and she closed the window. She was squeezing a scarf and she was resting her chin against her chest and trembling. The cold air filtered inside somehow. I was hankering for a cigarette, but my hands were numb and clutched at the steering wheel.

"We're almost there," she said calmly. She looked at me in the mirror until I continued paying attention to the road.

I could hear a noise like that of something sucking and struggling to get out of the box. I slowed down. The midget leaned against the box, squeezing it with his stumpy and strong arms as if they were lobster pincers. The old woman said something in a hushed voice and looked at the box with tenderness.

"Stop at the corner," Baby Jane commanded.

I parked. The midget was having a rough time controlling the box, which was shaking. He seemed like a defiant yet bullied child willing to do anything to hold on to his toy, even if it meant his death. I looked at him almost with sympathy. They quickly got out of the car. She thanked me with a dismissive tone while helping the midget with the box, which had become heavier and more difficult to handle. They set the box down and something inside was desperately stirring. Charley immediately hugged Baby Jane's waist. She calmed him by patting his rosy cheeks, and then she pushed him away in an offhand manner. Charley approached my car door.

"Take care. Thanks." He said this in Spanish and tossed two crumpled fifty-dollar bills onto the backseat. Then he wiped the tears from his face with the back of his hand, and he returned for the box.

They slowly carried it to a three-story building with a doorman out front. I got out of the car to close the rear windows and check if they had left anything that could get me tangled up. I didn't find my baseball bat beneath the seat. I had forgotten it at the station. I was aching for a beer and to give them a good thrashing. I could see the doorman open the door for them; he then wrote something in a small notebook that he had on his desk. I sat on the hood and lit a cigarette, which I let dangle from my lips. The embers burned like the fuse on a stick of dynamite. The warmth from the engine soothed my ass cheeks. The smoke seemed to be absorbed by a vacuum cleaner. There was no one around, not even raccoons. I made my hands into fists, as they were burning from the chill. I took out my gloves from my jacket's pockets and put them on. I looked up at the top floor; there were some lights on behind a floral curtain. The old woman and the midget were probably there; all the other windows were dark. I looked inside the car to find the fifty-dollar bills on the backseat that could accommodate three people. There they were, like some small detail lost in a Hopper painting. I picked them up. A taxi would have charged almost the same just for one trip. I turned on the high beams. If I hurried, I would have enough time for a couple more drinks in Port Chester. Rebeca.

I looked for a pay phone but I couldn't find any until I reached a parking lot at a Chinese restaurant. Once again, I took off my gloves to check my pockets, but I had no change. I took out one of the bills, and I shook it, showing it to the employee behind the counter. He looked at me with mistrust and immediately went to the kitchen. The lights inside the restaurant went off, one by one.

CHAPTER THIRTEEN

Night Shift at the Greenwich Mobil

The Mobil gas station. The enormous lit sign could be made out from any convergent point to the train station; the train would pass by, roaring over the town. Interstate 95 ran alongside the tracks all the way down the East Coast.

In order to get access to that route, or to enter Greenwich, one needed to go under the bridge and avoid a long roundabout to neighboring towns. "A sweetheart in every port," so goes the maritime saying, and "at every bridge, a gas station," is what could be described as the norm in the portside suburbs of the state. Driving up north from New York, one would feel an agreeable stirring of ants in the stomach upon facing the Atlantic chill on the sudden curve heading to Greenwich. If one continued on the elevated highway, through the clearings in the woods, one would see vistas of sea and sky. The gas station, one of the town's oldest landmarks, embodied the ideal of customer service, with client and employee living in harmony: ruddy gringos whom we were to admire and respect. We were their humble servants. Norman Rockwell could have easily spent some time there, gathering inspiration for the *Saturday Evening Post*.

I was in charge of the night shift, and I had become another tool in that service station with a repair shop. My shift was from five P.M. to midnight. Some assistants whom the manager hired during the two years that I worked there would help me out until ten P.M. They almost always fled back home to their countries during winter to avoid the freezing temperatures; they would stay there until April, when they would return looking for temporary jobs. Sometimes they would get canned for any reason. This would give Mike the time to revise the payroll and offer the minimum wage of $5.50, along with the promise that the pay would increase gradually to $8, as long as the new employee stayed on the job for two winters.

On average, the veterans ended up earning seventy-five cents more per hour, as the others were incapable of crossing the threshold into the subzero temperature, which proved to be intolerable starting around mid-November, right when their homesickness for the homeland turned them into deserters, a result of winter depression. More than mere assistants, they were my puppets, my accomplices, my henchmen, and my evening bile. Once we got past the pleasantries, we conspired in a greedy collaboration to grab some extra dollars from the services that weren't monitored by inventory or credit card sales. This generally revolved around plugging a tire, charging batteries, or the sale of small parts. Always splitting the profit. I would punch his card so that my "assistant" could leave one hour before finishing his shift, and so I could rule over the deserted place. The manager would leave every day at four o'clock, trusting in the doglike fidelity of the day laborers he would sniff out for each night at the local station. He was especially trusting of two Brazilians: Eudis and Josué. All the while they claimed to loathe Mike; they imitated him, such as his expressions and gestures. They watched everyone without missing a detail, despite the fact that no one spoke to them. They would come inside to talk to the clients as if they were the owners, ready to offer unsolicited help. They learned this from Mike, who always brownnosed the rich and Bob's children. Eudis would kiss the silver cross dangling from his neck whenever someone gave him a tip or when he received the envelope with his paycheck. Josué spent around seventy dollars each week on long-distance cards he would buy from the gas station; he would call his wife and father to check on a business they were starting with the money he sent home: a beachside soccer field.

"Fatty doesn't like *você*," Josué—referring to Mike—would let me know each time we passed each other while he ended his shift and I was about to start mine.

For those of us who worked at night, we would steal and loaf around as much as possible, which wasn't a lot, to be honest, and we complained about everything. Success consisted in not calling too much attention to yourself and in not messing up and turning your accomplice into an involuntary informer who would get you fired, or force you to replace the missing goods. We felt giddy whenever we pocketed the dough, and we would scrutinize each other, to check if there was some evidence that should be hidden.

Sometimes I would ask my coworker to bring me a bottle of whiskey from the nearby liquor store before going home. I liked to discreetly drink from behind the counter while watching the night absorb the highway's din. After ten, the white light inside and by the service area would keep me company. The train's horn traveling to New York City or New Haven would sound off each thirty minutes. From time to time, a worker would come to the station in order to put a few dollars' worth of gas into his tank, just enough to reach one of the towns nearby that was cheaper. When the clientele diminished, I would cross the street to get tea or coffee from my neighbor working at the Texaco. The two gas stations, along with five other stations, were a chain belonging to Bob, a puny, haughty, and standoffish gringo who acted as such to avoid any requests for more than a dollar's raise each year. He collected show cars, and he would cruise around the city limits in his red '57 Chevy convertible as if he were the town marshal. He and Mike wore short-sleeved shirts and neckties, even in winter. A cautious guy, Bob would enter the Mobil station through its enormous driveway, and he would lock himself up in the office to go over sales receipts with his lackey. When they wrapped things up, Bob would instruct us to revere the workplace while sizing us up, and then he would teach us some interesting facts about the business before crossing the street as if he were about to fight in a duel.

Bob gave jobs, but he never took care of giving raises. He left that to Mike, who was always wiping sweat from his brow with a handkerchief whenever in the presence of his boss. Mike rudely gave orders to whoever was nearby while looking into his notebook, a cigarette deeply entrenched in his mouth. He liked to show off, strutting from one end of the station to the other, taking care of minor problems with a smile and cracking a joke, receiving the gratitude of the clients, often while he scolded the employees. Who but Mike could possess the Ten Commandments of Customer Service? He would quickly recite them, respectful of the procedures they listed, which had never failed him after twenty-five years of putting them to good use every day, and he would do this like a preacher who raises his Bible and recites from memory some verse that best illustrates the sin that was committed and how to pardon it. Bob and Mike, who never took the time to learn about Charles Dickens, could have been Mr. Bounderby and Mr. Gradgrind in Coketown, rigorously in pursuit of norms and concrete facts. Empirical Taylorists, applying to life what Frederick Taylor had promoted as "scientific management." No room for improvisation in a business devoted to "mechanics." If this was not so, then why all the tools, the diagrams, the tune-ups, adjustments? If not, then what were the inventories, the time cards, the monthly performance sheets? They knew this better than anyone. They were a source of pride for those with working-class roots. The town of Greenwich had seem them grow and struggle just like their parents and grandparents. They were the finest example of "do it on your own." No one gave them any handouts. It was all due to hard work, to saving up money, and to staying loyal. *"Isn't that so, Eudis?!"*

Mike would leave the envelope with my pay next to the gas pumps, in the panel for cash payments, and he would almost always leave a memo stapled to my time cards. He knew that I, like everyone else, despised him, but I had little contact with him, apart from a few minutes on Saturday, when I would get to work an hour earlier, and he would be there, giving his orders so that no one would call him about problems at work during the weekend.

On holidays, he arranged for there to be one person working the night shift. If I had any bones to pick with Mike, it had to be done through the Brazilians. They presumed that they could influence the decisions of their boss, and whenever the occasion arose, they would let him know about our gripes. It was through Eudis that I found out Mike was upset because during my free times, I didn't personally inform him of any problems that would put the prestige of the business into peril.

That was another way of bursting that potbelly's liver. I started to write detailed messages about everything that wasn't working properly: dripping faucets, paint stains on walls, busted buckets and trash cans, overtime that he had not included in my latest paycheck, tools that needed to be replaced, phone numbers of clients asking for an estimate, messages from friends and acquaintances, memos about customers who were upset about petty shit. I would place these memos into the envelopes with money that I would slip into the safe that was hidden behind a bright calendar bearing the logo of a repair shop. I later learned from Eudis that Mike would rip up my messages without reading them. One of the tasks belonging to the night shift was to make sure the cash and IOUs didn't accumulate in the cash register. It was necessary to place them in dated envelopes and arrange cash by their value, making sure they were stacked faceup. The safe was behind Mike's desk, and as soon as he finished balancing the books the next morning, he would send one of the two Brazilians to the bank with a bag filled with cash, checks, deposit slips.

"Hello."

"Hello."

That's what our face-to-face encounters on Saturdays consisted of when Mike slowly walked to his truck next to the gas pumps and then hit the road. Sometimes he would wait for Eudis to run over and fill his gas tank. I didn't look at them. My attention was focused on the avenue, waiting for a car to signal that it would make a pit stop. The unique and most important benefit I enjoyed was not having to feel Mike's halitosis on my neck.

There were moments I envied my neighbor's position at the Texaco. He watched the night pass, every night of the year, from within his booth with a tinted window. He controlled everything on a computer, and he never had to pump gas for anyone or talk. His job didn't include getting drenched in the rain or freezing during winter. If there was a problem with the pumps, he only had to call the maintenance service and then go home. If there was a problem with a client, he could give instructions through a microphone in a squeaky English that put your nerves on edge.

At the Mobil station, one would have to ask why the pumps never failed during storms, especially during blizzards. When the temperature dropped to fifteen below, the line of cars extended way past the two entry points to the station. There was never a lack of prudent drivers who decided to stock up on things "just in case." I had to invent answers to their endless questions about mechanical problems and then advise them to go to the crooked service station, which was open for business during the morning; I had to play the role of a road map and invariably converse with drivers who hadn't spoken to anyone else all day, especially old people and insomniacs. I loved helping out retirees who seemed to have stepped out of a sitcom. Lost on the highway, they sought a decent hotel, and I would send them to Exit 5, some miles farther north, in the black neighborhood close to where I lived.

The gas prices at the Mobil varied little from the other gas stations in the town, but its "old-time" nostalgic air attracted clients. All of this, as well as our poor salaries and our relationship with Mike, gave us employees of both the night shift and day shift a sense of belonging to something. We feigned that we were all team players working toward the same goals, and we would complain about the workplace and the pay in the same way we would about the change in weather each new season. We were a prime example of what more tolerant bosses, especially those who were "politically correct," would call "diversity." That made it easier for them to fuck us over. Mike's zeal over our work performance was equal to the flattery he gave Bob, who greedily cooked the books at the two stations. During his years as a manager, he had learned all the ins and the outs of the business, including our petty thievery, which he would ignore so that the worker with the least amount of time on the job could get enough experience. Then he would fire the thief. My turn was fast approaching.

Visiting the Texaco at night was a routine that I had followed since the start of my employment. The two gas stations were on the corners across from the train station, which was the only station for miles around where no one was allowed to sleep on the platform benches. The workday was going well; I hadn't attended to any clients for an hour and a half. Greenwich wasn't what one could call a town with any nightlife. Just getting a cup of tea involved pinching awake the dozing clerk.

My neighbor was a Hindu in his fifties, and if he wasn't smiling spastically, I would catch him sleeping or reading a prayer book on his lap with incomprehensible letters, his eyes going from right to left. He would start work at ten at night, and he would finish at six in the morning. He would let clients pay inside until eleven; afterward, he would conduct his business from behind a bulletproof window. I would know about his sales because of the speaker he used. Light would strike his ashen face. The shelves behind him were filled with candy, maps, and parts and the refrigerator with beverages, and the general air of abandonment seemed carefully inventoried.

A taxi driver was complaining about the price of cigarettes and it being a slow night while he paid. His gripes could have continued indefinitely, like a taxi's meter that ticks off the increasing tariff of tedium, but the driver left, and the Hindu blessed him with his eternal smile of a boy tired of behaving well. That grimace ensured him a stable job and veiled his hatred for those working the day shift who sometimes would cover for him.

"How are you?" he greeted me without taking his eyes off the driver who was removing the nozzle from his car. He remained silent as if he was scared that the taxi driver could hear us through the bulletproof window. When the driver started his car, he cupped his hand over the microphone and said: "It's been busy tonight. I've sold a lot of cigarettes. What do you think?"

I asked for tea. Bob offered us free hot drinks during the winter. Clients had to pay a dollar per cup.

"Help yourself," he said, and he set his prayer book next to the cash registrar while he mumbled as he counted out the money that just came in.

All of a sudden, while I was looking at the Mobil station, a sense of anxiety entered me, and I wished to flee from the unforgiving winter. The blackened and dry firs seemed to have stiffened in a futile effort to reach sunlight, and the wind was stirring up whirlwinds of litter and snow. I liked dissolving my anxiety by thinking about the gas station as a small island suspended in the emptiness. The idea calmed me. The Hindu seemed wide-awake, so I decided to talk to him some more.

"Do you dream often?" I asked.

"Not always. Sometimes I can't remember what I dreamed. It's as if I had fallen asleep for only a second."

"I mean personal dreams, goals, plans for the future. Things you want to do, for example, like buying a new car, getting a house like the ones around here, obtaining your green card, I don't know, doing something with your life."

"Ah, of course. But I have to work very hard because my wife doesn't speak English. She wants to go to my country and the plane ticket is very expensive. You spend hours flying."

"Have you heard of the American Dream?"

"No. What is it?"

"To have everything you want and to be whatever you want to be."

"Really? I can't complain. I have a job and my wife is very happy in this country. We're going to buy a used car and she's going to learn how to drive. This will help us out because every morning I have to drive my children to school." And he opened his eyes wide, as if what he had just told me was written in his book of psalms. Then he shot the question back at me: "What is your dream?"

"You have to save up a lot of money, you understand me? It's going to be brutal here. I haven't slept well for days. I believe that now I'm even beginning to enjoy the films of Wes Craven."

"Who?" he asked.

The Hindu smiled. Despite everything. There were no dreams, only facts to share and bad jokes to pass some time with someone even simpler than I, and that wasn't of much help. I would have to read *The Great Gatsby* again. If there existed a latent myth in all of us, it was working perfectly: something that wasn't true, but that materialized every day while we paid for a hamburger or landed a new job for fifty cents more an hour.

No cars were coming to either of the gas stations. I could clearly hear the buzzing of the gigantic lamps above the Texaco pumps. In the distance, the Mobil station was turning into an enormous painting like one of those that they hang from the walls in diners and behind the front desk at auto shops. The gas stations were the wet nurses of twentieth-century progress. That's where the chronometer of change was nourished. My tea had become cold. All I could think of doing was scratching my head and humming a song. There was still an hour and a half before it was time to close shop. I still had to take inventory of the oil, close the accounts, put everything in envelopes and deposit them into the safe, and sweep the floor of the shop, and then I could bring the trash to the bin, scrub off the grease from my hands with a detergent that had phosphorescent green grains, turn off the pumps and the lights, and punch out. It seemed like the whole town was asleep except for us two. Nothing to say, but...

"Have you heard of *The Great Gatsby*? It's a good story," I said while opening the door and leaving.

"No. What is it about?"

"It's about a bootlegger who becomes a millionaire, but who never marries the woman of his dreams because she falls in love with a man who, apart from being rich, is an aristocrat."

The euphoria prior to the Great Depression as a meta-phor for arrivistes, and which allowed the most pres-umptuous to make their fortunes. But Gatsby lacked the nihilism necessary to laugh at the snubs coming from his lover, or to murder his enemies. In the end, Gatsby was nothing more than a bookish and scared ruffian brought to the world by way of a writer who would loathe interacting with someone like the character he had created. I delivered my review like one of those given by critics on the television before the movie starts.

"Ah, but there's a lot of cute women in this country, right? If you work hard and stay out of trouble, you can get one of them."

The Hindu showed me his enormous yellowish smile, and then he pointed his gaze across the street. At the pumps, a gorgeous black convertible had parked. Inside there were two blondes of the aerodynamic type. At last, I smiled.

"You're talking about one of them, right?" he concluded.

I returned running. The Hindu with the bland smile lived like a sleepwalker, while I lived in continuous déjà vu. The neon lights from the nearby businesses seemed intrusive in the soft penumbra of the street. Mobil immobile.

Luxury cars driven by local Gatsbys crossed the avenue, heading for the highway. No "Daisy" anywhere, thus there was no risk of death by being run over. A horn sounded from an Audi to greet the blondes. The successful residents of Greenwich: another concrete example of what was the American Dream. Well-being while traveling more than 70 miles per hour in brand-new European cars. In that kingdom walled off from the rest of the world by its property value, there was no room for insomniac greasers.

The blondes chattered while waiting. They brushed back their hair with their hands and gesticulated while speaking. When I reached them, the driver turned off the engine. The passenger looked through her purse while I asked what type of gas.

"The cheapest," she responded with the same smile that Daisy wore when she agreed to marry Tom Buchanan, Jay Gatsby's rival.

I pumped the gas like an automaton while thinking about what my neighbor, who wasn't missing a thing from his window, had said: "Work hard and stay out of trouble."

I finished, and Daisy handed me her American Express. She paid for five dollars' worth of the most expense gas around for miles. The heater inside the car was on high. I quickly scrutinized the girl's face, trying to find traces of her origin, and she returned my gaze with a look of annoyance before continuing her conversation with her friend, who was holding a leather change purse between her thighs, which were clothed in tight black velvet pants. *Okay, girls, let's get outta here.* My arms outstretched atop the leather backseat. Gucci shoes, Calvin Klein suit, silk Armani shirt. Coke, whiskey, and a bit of violence before the orgy taking place next to the pool. *Less Than Zero. That's who you are, fucker. Muster up the balls necessary and tell them to get out and pump their own gas. And then you can look at their asses. Hey, the tire looks a bit low; I think it might have a leak*—lean down, get closer—*do you hear it? No? well, I was just trying to help.* I charged them for the gasoline on the computer next to the pumps, and I returned the receipt signed to the name Lydia K. Majors, who looked at the copy before ripping it into pieces and tossing them out her open window.

The car started and a sweet odor of perfume vanished. *Get outta here and go run somebody down. There will always be someone who will take the blame for you.* I lit a cigarette and returned to the store. The night shift also served as a roadblock for all of those who were making layovers between their aspirations and who they really were: carpenters, house painters, cooks, maids, gardeners, medical assistants, security guards, file clerks, drivers, knaves, the unemployed, retirees, blacks, Asians, Latin Americans. They stopped at the gas station on their way to someplace, their jalopies teeming over with supermarket bags, crying children, clothing, furniture they had found in trash bins, good luck charms, and little cash. They were always in a hurry. Many of them were moving from one town to another. Some used the bathrooms, and it wasn't uncommon for them to clog the toilets.

I had thought up the Gatsby thing upon turning in a short essay in English class. The teacher said that I was "borderline," referring to my progress in class. I liked the adjective. It meant a lot. Mexican. Every day, hordes from all parts of the globe were arriving in search of their piece of the dream. Many found it at a job like mine. For others, *la migra* woke them up before it was time, like when one falls from the bed and wakes up, noticing that the television has been left on. What I am, what I was, and what I was used to being: someone who got in the way of others who were choosing to believe in the myths. To be violently shaken awake was part of the dream as well. I'm neither a believer nor blind. I could never be a Gatsby.

Midnight. Time to close up shop. The Hindu would have to keep on working. I was going home first. My consolation, daytime. I was tired, but I wanted to get a drink. I would go to sleep soon, hopefully, and I would dream.

CHAPTER FOURTEEN

In which...someone gets fired and someone new appears...
Diana Ross makes her own appearance...the Artist
learns about Carlos the Uruguayan.

We could look no farther north. We had reached the Arcadia of well-being. There was nothing left. We expiated for our greed with two-bit jobs. We were the martyrs of luxury, and we had turned as bourgeois as any fickle office clerk who has grown complacent with his love handles while watching videos alongside his family. The civilized zone of New England kept us free from the grip of immigration agents; it offered ESL classes and workshops. If we proved to be neither ill-intentioned nor disloyal, and if we blindly accepted its boring and peaceful puritanism and the superiority complex of its residents, they would smile at us and offer more work. Our prayers brimmed over with a love for the dollar.

My telephone rang. I was boiling some pasta to go with a T-bone and steamed asparagus. It was Mike from the station. "I need you here immediately; we've got some major problems."

"Sorry, but I don't start until four, and that's if the blizzard will let me. What's up?"

"Fine then. You have a new coworker. *Maybe you know why*."

And he hung up. It was simple: someone got fired.

The Brazilians instructed the new man, Carlos, as though the daily routine at work required great skill. At five sharp, they ran to their cars, freezing. From inside the station, Carlos and I watched the line of cars waiting for gas. The Brazilians joked and waved at us from behind their fogged windshields. Silently, we walked outside into the snowfall. The wind hissed like a sirocco. Carlos spoke to me only to let me know that he was going to the bathroom at a moment when we didn't have time to even place the valves back into the pumps.

He came back bristling with energy, trying to pep himself up. He barely said a word, and he did his work easily, as if the snow that he shoveled didn't weigh a thing and there was no danger of breaking our necks after slipping on a patch of ice. Carlos wiped windshields clean of mud and salt, remained friendly by joking with the drivers—the absolute opposite of myself, especially when it came to answering questions about the cost of different repairs or when I was asked to check the oil. The cold had frozen my sense of humor until summer.

After nine, almost as if the town had signed a pact, the cars would arrive after lengthy stretches of no activity, so that their appearance was preferable to the freezing night's tedium.

I offered a smoke, but Carlos politely declined and then he took out his own pack from his jacket. He took a long drag on a mentholated cigarette, held his breath, and then, after a few seconds, exhaled through his nose. The dense puff offered a clear testimony to his addiction. He kept quiet and did nothing to come across as friendly. Carlos didn't take his eyes off the clock, and at ten on the dot, he took off his cap, which had left deep impressions on his temple.

"See you tomorrow," he said softly while walking to his car, which I had seen before but didn't know was his. I had guessed that a tow truck had left the car, a gray-and-blue BMW.

A week later the car didn't start, and he pushed it behind the shop to hide it from Mike. He made a quick phone call and waited smoking by the telephone. After a while, a white

Galaxie with tinted windows appeared outside the station's cab. The passenger door opened, and Carlos immediately got in, forgetting to punch out. I did it for him.

$

Diana Ross lived on a hill overlooking a cove a mile away from the service station. She kept an open tab with Mobil. I feigned disinterest, but Mike and the other employees all rushed to tend to her.

One of her cars was driven by a young religious Colombian. He would pull up to the station twice a week, almost always at night, after having finished his daily rounds transporting the diva's personnel. He would get out to stretch and shake our hands without taking his eyes off the pump and the gallons ticking away. This particular Holy Roller looked like a game show host: he sported a tie, suit, and nice manners. "Thank the Lord" was always on the tip of his tongue. Sometimes, if it was a Sunday, and he was accompanied by his fiancée (who behaved primly, as though the pastor were watching), he wore a polo shirt and dark glasses. He never tired of praising the advantages he enjoyed from his job as a family chauffeur. He also never coughed up a tip, and he would size us up while bragging how his attractive boss was a clone of Michael Jackson. We would fill up his tank, check the oil and tire pressure. When he signed the bill, he would bless us. I always suspected that he was pilfering small amounts from petty cash reserved for tips. He was fired a year later, and he never said why. He got a job as a limo driver, waiting for clients, driving back and forth from the airport. He continued to fill his tank at the Mobil station, but his attitude changed. He no longer greeted us, and he contemptuously requested our services, yet no longer got out of his car. However, he would check the air pressure by walking around his car and kicking the tires. His black suit and tie, as wrinkled as the dollars he handed us, made him look insignificant and vulgar.

A gigantic black man transported Mrs. Ross around in a black limousine. Every two weeks, the tinted window would lower just enough so we could glimpse the mummy in the backseat: sunglasses, sparkling black dress, fluffy coiffure, and makeup that looked like a mortician had caked it on her face prior to her attendance at a gala dinner in the wax museum. The bodyguard also wore sunglasses, and he would sweep us aside with a glance. Without saying a word, he took it for granted that his scowl and the gas door clicking open were enough for us to understand that we had to fill the tank. While I wiped the windshield and rear window, Carlos ran to the pump and stuck in the nozzle, switching the pump's trigger to automatic, all while simulating a quickie. We assumed that the bodyguard wasn't looking at us in the rearview mirror. Carlos ground his hips, thrilled about the thrashing we'd get before losing our jobs, all because of the buffoonery that I had taught him.

Every three visits, after paying off the tab scribbled on a whiteboard, the bodyguard would pull the limousine up a few feet, and through a crack in the rear window, two bony fingers, sometimes gloved, would extend a couple of one-dollar bills.

$

Carlos spoke English well; he had learned it on the streets. His fluency calmed me, because this meant that there would be no misunderstandings when it came to customer service.

He liked joking around with the black guys, mimicking their way of speaking and gesturing when in their presence, acting like it was the most natural thing. Even when there was nothing to do, he would walk around the station, keeping himself busy with improvised tasks that wouldn't keep him far from the front counter. At least once during every shift, he would get on the phone and speak excitedly about a soccer match or make a date to meet at some bar in Port Chester after work.

After a few days, we found a way to appreciate each other's presence and to ignore our mutual mistrust. We shared frank stories from our past, of our wanderings in the United States, comparing our errant ways. Our loneliness ached, and it was best to massage it with pride. We studied each other— our bond wasn't weakened by that mixture of gratitude and greed that makes day laborers submissive.

Carlos reached the United States with a group of Uruguayans who spent six months in Nuevo Laredo, wandering the border with passports lacking visas, and several additional months in a detention center in Texas, until someone within the network of countrymen got him a family request from Rhode Island. Money for the paperwork was wired from Uruguay, and he found himself a free man traveling to New York in a bus, joined by some of his friends who'd found themselves in the same circumstance. After eight years, everyone—except for Carlos—had saved money and landed jobs that were not as physically demanding. Carlos experienced plenty of unforgettable adventures, among them when he worked in a hovel sucking off older men with respectable appearances. One of them turned out to be his brother-in-law—twenty years older than his sister—who was on a supposed business trip. Carlos discovered this after the fact, when he received a letter from his sister accompanied by a photo. He lived alone almost always, changing rooms and towns constantly. He knew the area well, and he would recommend bars, massage parlors, or rooms that were being rented out for cheap.

One night I decided to reveal my flask. At that moment we stopped viewing each other as strangers who discover a dollar bill and try to wait for the perfect moment to snatch it first. After his third swig, Carlos left to help a client while taking little leaps and shimmying his shoulders like a center back jogging onto the field to relieve a teammate.

"Life is beautiful," he'd say to remember some passage from his experiences. His constant euphoria made me guess at the secret to his optimism: every night we would take turns picking up some Chilean wine, beer, or whiskey. The first time we smoked marijuana deep within the mechanic shop, Carlos quickly revealed himself to be a poet:

"This is life: to be at ease no matter where."

We spoke slowly, without pausing, to save up enough energy to laugh in the faces of the clients when they handed back the receipts.

"Things look great!" Carlos would frenetically shout whenever an elderly couple, or housewives, or hippies, or a car with plates from a different state, pulled into the station. We ran out to the pumps, making ourselves look obliging. I would distract the driver with questions about the last time he had an oil change or when his next tune-up was due. I would clean the windows and then ask the driver to open the hood; I would pretend that I was checking the fluids. While this was going on, Carlos would use a key to loosen up the tire's air valve, supposedly while checking the pressure. Once the tank was full, he would ask the client to park by the air compressor.

"I think you've got a leak," he would say with well-rehearsed concern.

"That's impossible, I checked them before leaving," the untrusting prey would claim, now in a bad mood, as he would have to get out and suffer the cold weather.

"Take a look for yourself," I would add.

Carlos would fetch the mechanical jack and the patch kit, which included a powered lug wrench. From the entry of the mechanic shop, he'd guide the car inside. It was like a Formula 1 team. The prey reluctantly agreed to wait in the shop, unless there really was a leak; if so, we would let him observe the entire procedure. We would remove the tire and submerge it into a bucket of filthy and foul-smelling water and, after a few seconds, to give the bubbles a chance, Carlos would remove with pliers a nail or piece of glass that was merely stuck between the grooves. The price for checking the tire: ten dollars. Fifteen dollars when we weren't lying. This paid for dinner and the drunkenness that helped us endure our shift.

CHAPTER FIFTEEN

**In which...the Artist tussles with the homies...
plots his escape...plays cards with Fredson.**

Noon on a Sunday. From west to east, going downhill, Railroad Avenue stretched 382 yards until it reached its edge, the traffic light at the intersection with Greenwich Avenue. That's where downtown ended: next to the highway and the railroad tracks. The slope was steep and cars could reach delirious speeds if they didn't pump their brakes. The parking spots along the sides of the road, which were always taken on either side, barely left any room for pedestrians or joggers, who dashed for the sidewalk farther ahead like bullfighters diving behind the wooden barriers.

To go uphill, one needed a well-tuned engine as well as courage, for when a speeding car appeared up ahead, at the summit, which was barely sixteen feet across. From there, I would coast down the steep incline until it reached the Texaco and Mobil stations at the corner and the public parking lot.

On workdays, long caravans formed as they waited for the traffic light to turn green; that helped avoid constant skidding or rushing into the Mobil as if they wanted to run over the workers. But on weekends—especially on Sundays—a car on the hilltop would rev its engine before making its descent, interrupted only if the traffic light turned red before it reached the intersection. This rumble drowned out the creaking from the firs and pines being swayed by the high winds. It seemed sometimes like a demon was hunkered within the foliage, attracting prey with its gruff whistling. It was supernatural and disconcerting, and it became the herald of an unforgiving fate.

I would kill time while some aged traveler or families on their way to Sunday activities stopped at the Mobil for gas or directions. The hill divided the legendary prosperity of those living in the town from the poverty of those living on the outskirts. In those areas there were multifamily homes inhabited by mainly black and Latino workers employed in the neighboring bread factory, whose production was distributed in Connecticut, New York, and New Jersey. Continuing west, Railroad Avenue ended at a fork in the road, leading to either Manhattan or Port Chester. According to many clients coming to the gas station, the acidic, sharp odor of exposed trash didn't come from the factory, but from the skunks and inhabitants of the multifamily homes.

A family of quarrelsome homies lived in those narrow and poorly ventilated apartment buildings on the curve that led to Port Chester. The kids continuously came down to the Mobil to put air into their bicycle tires and basketballs or to get some junk food. It was tough for them to tone down their posturing when they had to ask me for money or help turning on the air pump. During those moments they joked around with me as if we were friends. They had ruthless gazes and cute faces, like small, wild animals ready to bite. Like all the kids who went to the gas station, they viewed me as someone beneath them on the totem pool, someone whom they could trample as they wished.

Once night fell, they waited for the moment when I had to pump gas. I didn't have enough time to rush in and stop them from entering as a mob, shaking the cigarette machine. There was no use trying to tell them they were underage and couldn't buy the stuff. Anyway, they'd accuse the machine of taking their money, and then they'd demand that I return it. Ignoring them, I avoided their insistence on me giving them spare change or on reimbursing them for the pack of cigarettes. It would have been like throwing bread crumbs to seagulls.

Once, my negativity riled up their tall and lanky leader. He challenged me to a fight, and when I tried to push him away from a blow's distance, he took out a handgun from his pants. I couldn't be certain if it was real, but my fear convinced me it was. Behind him, his girlfriend distracted me, as she was showing off her enormous and firm breasts beneath a leotard. She wore no bra. With her arms crossed, she chewed gum, licking her red, carnal lips. No way to even place a hand on her. After hiding the weapon, they ran off, accusing me of being a pervert, racist, child abuser, and all manner of things that thieves shriek whenever someone puts them in their place.

$

A couple months before I had a similar experience. Carlos was arguing with a geezer dressed up in golf clothes who had refused to pay for the gas. According to the old guy, he had said *"Five,"* but Carlos understood *"Full,"* and he filled up the tank. Carlos was sure that he was being tricked and he called the police. The trickster with sleep-yellowed eyes shouted that we had swindled him and that he would tell other customers that we had discriminated against him. Carlos and I took turns attending to customers and arguing with the lunatic. While he was moving his jalopy to park it in front of the mechanic shop, the old man seemed like one more grifter trying to pull off his usual scam. When he got out of his car to confront us, his hulking frame convinced me that we needed urgent help.

When it arrived, the patrolman told us to stop all service and for us three to follow him to a corner outside the restrooms. With his back turned to the gas pumps, he listened to the allegations of each party, nodding as he listened to the old man's lies but interrupting Carlos and me when we told our version, reminding us that we weren't *Americans*, and by doing so, he was insinuating that we were working without papers. In the end, he asked for our information to fill out a report, and he let the old man leave after he had paid five dollars. We kept on working for the rest of the day, punished by the justice system of a nation that stubbornly denies its caste society. With our usual ways to earn some extra cash, we covered the losses of that embezzlement.

My coworker Neal was with me when I had the argument with the armed homie. He came running to separate us, and he took him to the corner, spoke to him, and gave him some change so that he would leave. The following days, Neal was nervous and on edge. The troublemaker would pass by on the sidewalk accompanied by his girlfriend, and he would threaten me by pointing at me with his index finger. Railroad Avenue nourished paranoid and defiant hatreds and could rile anyone.

$

From my spot, I held on to that moment in which two older homies quickly pedaled their bicycles without brakes halfway up the hill to then let themselves go down at top speed, feeding their hunger for a thrill. Usually, one of the younger kids rode on the handlebars. The challenge was to cross the intersection in such a way that neither the cars going along Greenwich Street nor the red light forced the rider to put the soles of his sneakers against the rear tire, creating a makeshift and buzzing brake. The rest of the gang followed after them, shouting euphorically, and the final rush of adrenaline burst out when the kamikazes reached their goal: the entrance ramp to the Rolls-Royce dealership next to the Texaco. That's where the others waited their turn.

Although they ignored me, I clapped when they returned. Some pedaled their bicycles with their bodies stretching ahead, others seated, and all of them boasting. Pedestrians and drivers gaped as if they were an invasion of ragged and panting zombies.

Then I returned to my duties.

$

Inside the station's cab I frantically went over my finances. Over and over again, I added up the same amount it would take for me to leave the United States. I had no other reason to be here, apart from stubbornness. I'd saved up enough to seek out other hills and slopes to keep me entertained. Through the window, I gazed at the enormous firs across the street. They had grown greener since March thanks to the occasional drizzle that sometimes turned into sleet. The trees poured their shade across the parking lot in front of the train station. As the hours went by, the nose-diving flights of seagulls turned daring, and their cawing thundered louder as the trash bins filled up with the remainders from lunch. From roofs, branches, and power cables, the flocks of swallows waited for their opportunity. They were also way up high, like shots from a shotgun bouncing from one side of the blue sky to the other.

I didn't intend to say farewell to anyone or thank my numerous employers like so many others did on such occasions. Eudis told the costumers about his departure for Brazil a month in advance after having worked there for ten years. His scheme was to receive some fat tips as a reward for having been such an accommodating gas station attendant. When they found out, management immediately fired him, preventing any embezzlement or loss in their inventory of parts and tools. To get enough to pay for his flight, Eudis had to sell some of the gifts he was planning to bring to his family, as he had cleaned out his savings and was relying on his final paychecks and bonuses.

Mike knew what I was up to, but he played dumb, as that was a pleasure no one could deny him. He'd wait until early the next morning, that moment when he'd screw his fat ass into the chair next to his desk, and while balancing the books, he'd decide to *not* overlook one of my petty embezzlements. Then he'd contact one of the many people on his waiting list, and then he'd call for me. But for the moment, I was the one calling the shots. And if he even thought of calling me, no one would answer the phone. Norma, upset with my decision to leave, had canceled service and moved out. We got rid of everything possible at a garage sale; what we couldn't sell, we gave away or tossed into the trash. All in one weekend.

I didn't intend to return my work uniform. It gave me a certain pleasure, a mixture of pride and pain, to hold on to it. I wanted it always in reach as a reminder about what I did to earn a few bucks, like some "tough guy" who would really never be anything more than a poor devil. I entertained the idea of robbing all the cash available during the weekend. It would be nice to slip the dated envelopes filled with coupons, receipts, and loose change into the safe, but without any cash. But my loathing for this job was worth much more and couldn't be paid off. In the end, I grabbed a hundred bucks from the safe for taxi fare to the airport. Call it a modest "compensation." When Mike realized the missing amount, my airplane would be taking off.

I hoped to return to New York one of these days. The FBI had bigger fish to fry.

$

Fredson hums while raking and watering the small gardens that mark off the property belonging to the Mobil station. Going beyond could mean getting fired, according to the rule that specifies abandoning one's post. Fredson forgets about the time on the clock and the rule that doesn't apply to him. A few hours remain before he will set off to the county hospital. He takes care of invalids. The other two Antilleans who work at the gas station do the same. Fredson spends the majority of his time at work tinkering with his brand-new red Honda—he gets his tools ready before going under the hood—while the ragamuffin music on his stereo booms loud enough to be heard on his native island. Fredson knows that that's how he gets the attention of female customers in order to flirt with them, as they also know how attentive he is. With his high voice and accent, it sounds like he is trying to accommodate dentures in his mouth while chatting to the clients about warmer climes, aphrodisiacs, and the power of his sports car.

Fredson has returned to the station's cab, taking advantage of the slow hours to play cards behind the counter. We'd learned to sympathize with each other, tolerating each other's shortcomings. True comrades.

He has no clue, but just out of sheer coincidence, he's the one who gets to hear my last story told at the gas station. It's less thrilling than zipping down the hill on a bicycle, but at least I get to turn down sharing his lunch of rice and oxtail stew.

CHAPTER SIXTEEN

In which...the Artist's father dies, as told to Fredson.

My mother died of an embolism at a private hospital. She didn't enjoy life much; she was always worried and running from one place to another. A few months later, her oldest son contributed to the decreasing members in our large family. He suffered a death worthy of coverage in a sensationalist tabloid: a Molotov cocktail exploded in the crowded brothel where he was hanging out. We learned in detail about the pyromaniac through newspaper reports, while we visited the forensics lab and then the funeral home. Tragedies are the only inheritance that the poor never need to worry about losing.

My father endured his sadness for nine years, while diabetes slowly destroyed him and a foot developed gangrene and made him bedridden. When we visited him, he quickly pretended that it wasn't so. The stench betrayed his horror of having a limb sawed off, which is what finally happened after drawn-out and depressing visits to doctors' offices and public hospitals for the poor, filled with what seemed like the victims of the plague or some war. The people there would die alone and in silence, without cries for help or scandals. That's what convinced my older brothers to admit him to a private hospital where at least he would have a room to himself.

My oldest sister, Irene, was the only one with money in the bank. She financed the debts accumulated by others and arranged for her father-in-law to take over the mortgage of another sister. Irene had been waiting for our old man to kick the bucket in order to also scoop up my parents' house. Her wish was granted a year later: my father died from a heart attack while being pushed in a wheelchair in the hospital he was visiting for a routine check-up after an operation. Irene was always business minded, and she figured out how to hold on to the plot of land and the house without anyone complaining.

I was still working as a messenger at a bank and Ricardo was working as a deliveryman. The younger siblings never got it into their heads that they could have helped out with paying the debts of their elder siblings. I'm not chiding them. Ricardo and I were hungry and wild. We would follow the latest developments in the family from offstage. Of all of my father's idiosyncrasies, we clearly inherited his overbearing pride, which undermined the best intentions of his family.

For me, traveling was merely a dream provoked by reading and cinema. I filled up some of my free time by writing for newspapers and magazines. I would read adventure novels, the crime sheets, and essays on art and criminality. Minimum wage, tuna or sardines with bread rolls, oatmeal, beer and menus from a greasy spoon, a portable typewriter, few ambitions, slutty girls who pretended they were respectable but were addicted to drugs and mooching, a stupid and insolent pride dressed up like the Ramones, and interminable ramblings on foot, by metro, and the cheapest bus lines filled me with anxiety. An insane and erratic anxiety, one that rendered me incapable of fighting for what I wanted. It was a terrifying feeling that sought refuge in a room in the slums, among others like myself.

$

After my father's foot was removed, Irene looked after him in her house in a snazzy neighborhood (which was worth at least a hundred amputations). I just tried to say things that would keep his chin up, without embarrassing him. Even in his wheelchair, he could do things without any help. Still, we all looked after him, and we would excuse his outbursts. He even had a maid who would wipe his ass after he crapped. But he was filled with resentment, and his endless hubris made it so he would hide his fear. For the first time in his life, he was on the lookout for death. His prescriptions forbade any drinking, and at Irene's house it was impossible to rebel against that without a fight, just as it was impossible to spend the evenings quietly drinking brandy while telling stories with the radio on and a large dog beside him.

There were moments in which circumstances made us feel united, as if we were all sentenced to serve time at a forced labor camp. Fed up, we finally turned our backs on each other. There was nothing left to do. The insulin took its place as the nurse of the grumpy bear, practically defeated by sugar.

During his convalescence, my father demanded to return to his house in case someone dared buy it. He had lived in a poor neighborhood teeming with riffraff, but he preferred to die there than put up with the litigious lodging provided by my sister and her husband. We anxiously hoped to see him like he once was: watering the flowerpots, checking out the noise on the street, shouting at the neighbors. *Ruff-ruff*, his dog barking at the gate, hungry. *Miaow*, his cat, Monkey, pattering along the ledge, waiting for someone to toss out a drumstick. *Prrrreeeeeee, prrreeeee*, the parrots shrieking in their filthy cages. *Currr, Currrr*, the pigeons flapping onto the patio to peck at stale bread crumbs. *Eeeeeee, eeeee*, the white rat in his cage shrieking, while growing and growing in a cage for canaries.

The old man's fighting cock was his love and pride. It fought against dogs and cats, and it would perch atop a small, stuffed lizard that was the table's centerpiece. The cock died in the jaws of a stray dog while my father was taking it for a stroll. I had left home from a very young age, but I would return whenever I lost a job and I had no other place to turn to and didn't have enough to scrape together for a deposit and first month's rent. I took advantage of those times to amble around the hood once again, hiding from the paddy wagons and the aggressive neighbors. I respected my father, but we didn't trust each other. He was jealous of my ambitious nature. We were too similar. Well, at least that's what my siblings said.

My father, like myself, possessed a rare gift for throwing away the things he loved most: money, prestige, friends. My mother threw him away as she died. Back then, I had no idea what it was like to live with a woman, but I really needed one all the time. And it was tough finding one who matched my tastes. Because of that, I read a lot at night. My father and I were two birds in the same cage, yet singing in different keys; scarred from each other's constant reproaches, we also shared some moments of true, mutual understanding. And after the death of my mother, we identified with each other even more.

$

Remembering my father seemed inevitable on that last Sunday at the gas station. Fredson was interested in the story. He didn't complain even as I reshuffled the cards without dealing them.

I didn't have the slightest idea of what had happened in the hospital that afternoon my father died. After I finished my shift at the bank, I went to visit Norma. I was carrying some manuscript draft I was hoping to revise that night, as if the only thing that mattered was to become a writer. Instead of Norma, the person I found there was Jesus, her arrogant and irascible husband, although a talented engraver whom I admired for his sincerity when it came to recognizing the thoroughly unlikable aspects of his character. Each time he had a show in a museum or gallery, he cast himself, with his meticulous creativity, further away from the daily grind and the passing admiration of others

Once his son walked out through the doorway, we spoke for a few moments until I could perceive his well-rehearsed coolness. What was coming next seemed predictable. But Jesus returned to being intense and eloquent with each serving of brandy and the passing of time, and nothing dramatic happened. I understood why when, without draining his glass, he filled mine to the brim.

"Your father just died," he told me, right when I was taking a sip. "Norma went to the funeral home to meet up with your brothers."

Drink it down or pour it out, as my father would say when it came to facing a problem. Jesus kept on informing me of the situation as if he were speaking about how to properly employ dyes, needles, and embroidery.

"Give me the address. I'm on my way," I demanded with the same tone, before finishing my drink with one swig.

All the while, his son was watching us as if we were two examples—in extreme opposite—of what he most feared being and what he hoped to be.

On the bus on the way to the funeral home, I was hounded by thoughts not necessarily related to my father. After his death, it was impossible for me to come to terms with the fact that I would never see him again. I had time enough to register it, but it wasn't enough; there is never enough time to accept the route to the worms. Meanwhile, from one neighborhood to the next, I realized that there was a blackout in the majority of the southern part of town, and that's where I was getting lost.

Exiting the bus, I walked along a darkened avenue, shred from time to time by the headlights of a passing car. With these shards of light, I made out a wall of volcanic rock. That's where I needed to go. I reached an iron door shaded by the glow of an emergency exit lamp. Before me, I saw the black masonry of a certain housing unit. It wasn't until then that I felt something. I felt lost in the vicinities of the mausoleum that housed the ashes of my mother and brother. I had to walk for a while in the darkness before coming across a public phone. I called my brother-in-law to double-check the address. (I didn't tell him where I was.)

Three hours later, I reached the funeral home downtown, facing a motel from which I had once rented a room and where I had stared out the window at the street. The bare legs of my girlfriend disappeared between the reflections and the passing traffic. They rested indifferently on the bed like a photo snapped by a forensics expert, while I mused upon life, death, and their unbreakable bond. It was a lie that we could liberate ourselves from that by fucking. My self-esteem was nourished by nonconformity and needs that were never satisfied. The ashtray stuffed with cigarette butts, at times, served as a participant in my restlessness. It was at that moment that I landed upon a motive to go and caress my girlfriend until she woke up. She opened her eyes and looked at her watch and said, alarmed, "Let's go. If not, we'll miss the last train."

I was on the opposite side now, trying to flow along with the cautious silence of my siblings. The poorly ventilated chapel was the larger of two other options. The coffin rested on two chairs with tall, red, velvet-covered backs beneath lamps with flame-shaped lightbulbs. Christ and crucifixes everywhere. It smelled of wax, cigarette smoke, and pine-scented air freshener. The tenuous incandescence allowed emotions to be emoted, freely or feigned.

The funeral home was filled with old crows who prowled around the open coffins, sometimes silently, and at other times competing loudly with each other, amping up their weeping or exaggerated looks of sorrow.

There was a lot of food in the other chapels, along with coffee, sweet rolls, and bottles of Bacardi, which the mourners would discreetly pour into cups. They couldn't stop from noshing on food and filling their paunches as if they were attending any normal social gathering. I decided it was best to stay next to my father and avoid the large patio that served as the general reception area. Over there, the tile floor was red and cracked. There were puddles everywhere and a faint stink of cheap perfume.

I didn't dare open the casket. I wanted to avoid the outpouring of sympathy accompanied by weeping, snot dripping from noses, and sappy comments about what a wonderful man my father was. They wouldn't have left me in peace. I sought silence. And now the old fellow couldn't help me frighten off anyone with his mordant quips about these very kind of occasions. In the morning, shortly before they cremated him, I scolded him for having involved us with this tedious process, so uncomfortable, so filled with people who had no sense of propriety and who were predisposed to enjoy the suffering that made his own children unable to go to sleep.

By the coffin's edge, I gazed at the street. People kept on coming and going, throwing a glance at the funeral home. A faint glow of motel-neon-blue glistened against the cars making their rounds, all of them with grime dripping down their chassis due to the drizzle. Weird noises were heard, almost as if enormous insects were gnawing at the ground beneath. My brothers wandered among the wakes to mourn for a business manager and an engineer who died drunk behind the wheel by smashing his car on the freeway. Then they addressed their own dearly departed, but ignored the mourners who were there to drink and grub on food.

My brother Francisco started to suggest some salsas for tacos; my sister Lucrecia listened to him and then followed his example by recommending some stews and recipes. Little by little, the rest of my brothers figured out the ironic requiem that the strangers were performing, and who felt at ease when they appeared to provide solidarity, as well as getting drunk and eating, until Francisco startled them by uttering a "no" with a tone that sounded more like "This is the final warning...!" The dinner guests left, feigning dignity by waiting for coffee and the rosaries in their own wake chapels.

All night, my attention was fixed on the coffin and the street. In the motel parking lot, cars came and went. I avoided greeting acquaintances. Later, I ran into my younger brother, Ricardo, deeper within the wake's gathering. He wept, unable to believe what had happened. I put my arm around his shoulders and reminded him that we had foreseen the end when, at night, we would find the old man on the sofa, facing the television, waiting for any noise from the front door, for brandy, for less boredom. "*Shhh*, don't wake him, he'll notice how wasted we are!"

His dog was so used to our schedule that he never barked when we entered. I would have liked to have returned to my father's house at that hour, if just to smell a ghost's cigarette, to gaze at the empty rooms, the tattered sofa, the king-size bed in disarray. The furniture broken, ready to be taken away. The spoils reserved for gravediggers, their beasts knowing that another hunger strike had ended.

Everything was leaving without leaving a trace of its ownership. Just like life.

EPILOGUE

I tore my time card in two before putting it back into its slot. I would have to take the train home, as I had sold my Toyota to the biggest asshole and ass-licker among the gas station attendants: Josué. He was the only one who had any money saved. The kamikazes on bicycles hunkered in, waiting for the right moment to run to the station cab and shake the cigarette machine.

I took advantage of Fredson going to the john to slip home and check on my flight by phone. Fredson knew what twelve years at the gas station meant to him. Many times, it meant taking care of things alone, all alone, during long Sundays and holidays. That's how he won the trust of Bob and Mike. There was no doubt that his neurosis was due to lack of sleep and a poor diet. Fredson lived an hour and a half from Greenwich, and four days a week his job at the hospital started at seven in the morning. Endless shifts of stretching and dozing behind the window of the gas station cab, as well as tough and monotonous work that he carried out quickly and without errors, without siphoning any extra cash. Fredson carefully thought about returning to his country. He knew very well about the misery and chaos he experienced as a child, and what he now had as a result of common sense and stubbornly sticking to his job.

That's what terrified me about Fredson. What difference was there between us if we both trod the same path paved by the same devils? There was nothing left to do. Fred would keep going down that path until he earned citizenship or Social Security. Not me.

Traveling is a way of flying away from myself and my memories. A charter was waiting for me in just a few hours.

BIOGRAPHIES

J.M. Servín is the author of eight books of fiction and nonfiction. He won the National Prize for Testimonial Writing in 2001 and the Fernando Benítez National Prize for Cultural Journalism in 2004. His novels, short story collections, and memoirs — including *For the Love of the Dollar* — have all been named books of the year by *Reforma* newspaper. He lives in Mexico City, where he coordinates the narrative journalism project Producciones el Salario del Miedo.

Anthony Seidman is a poet translator from Los Angeles. He is the author of three collections of poetry, including *Where Thirsts Intersect* and most recently, *A Sleepless Man Sits Up In Bed*. His work has been included in such journals as *Chiron Review, Nimrod, World Literature Today, Modern Poetry In Translation, Huizache, Cardinal Points,* and *The Black Herald,* among other publications. The Bitter Oleander Press recently published his new translation project, *Confetti-Ash: Selected Poems of Salvador Novo* with David Shook as his co-translator.

David Lida is the author of several books and most recently *One Life,* his critically acclaimed debut novel. His short story collection, *Travel Advisory,* was chosen by Barnes & Noble for their Discover Great New Writers program. *First Stop in the New World,* a street-level panorama of contemporary Mexico City, was hailed by the *New York Times,* the *Los Angeles Times,* and the *Chicago Tribune,* and chosen by the *San Francisco Chronicle* for its Best Books of the Year list. He lives in Mexico City.